SIDE BY SIDE

SIDE BY SIDE

Essays on Teaching to Learn

Nancie Atwell

The Center for Teaching and Learning
Edgecomb, Maine

HEINEMANN
Portsmouth, NH

IRWIN PUBLISHING
Toronto, Canada

HEINEMANN EDUCATIONAL BOOKS, INC.
361 Hanover Street   Portsmouth, NH 03801-3959
Offices and agents throughout the world

Published simultaneously in Canada by
IRWIN PUBLISHING
1800 Steeles Avenue West   Concord, Ontario, Canada L4K 2P3

A shorter version of "The Thoughtful Practitioner" first appeared in *Teachers Networking* 9, no. 3 (Spring 1989).

"A Special Writer at Work" appeared, in slightly different form, in *Understanding Writing: Ways of Observing, Learning, and Teaching K-8,* 2nd ed., edited by Thomas Newkirk and Nancie Atwell (Portsmouth, NH: Heinemann, 1988).

A shorter version of "Bringing It All Back Home" first appeared in *The New Advocate* 2, no. 1 (Winter 1989).

Other acknowledgments for borrowed material begin on page xi.

Every effort has been made to contact the copyright holders for permission to reprint borrowed material where necessary. We regret any oversights that may have occurred and would be happy to rectify them in future printings of this work.

Library of Congress Cataloging-in-Publication Data

Atwell, Nancie.
  Side by side : essays on teaching to learn / Nancie Atwell.
    p.   cm.
  Includes bibliographical references (p.).
  ISBN 0-435-08586-7
    1. Language arts—United States.   2. English language—Composition and exercises—Study and teaching—United States.   3. Reading—United States.   4. Cognitive learning—United States.   I. Title.
  LB1576.A795   1991
  428'.0071—dc20   91—6670
                                                                         CIP

Canadian Cataloguing in Publication Data

Atwell, Nancie
  Side by side : essays on teaching to learn
  ISBN 0-7725-1851-3

  1. Language arts.   2. English language—Composition and exercises—Study and teaching.   3. Reading.
  4. Cognitive learning.   I. Title.

  LB1576.A98   1991   428'.007'1   091-093831-8

ISBN 0-435-08586-7 (Heinemann)
ISBN 0-7725-1851-3 (Irwin/Canada)

Designed by Maria Szmauz.
Cover photo by Jo Haney.

Printed in the United States of America.
92 93 94 95 9 8 7 6 5 4 3 2

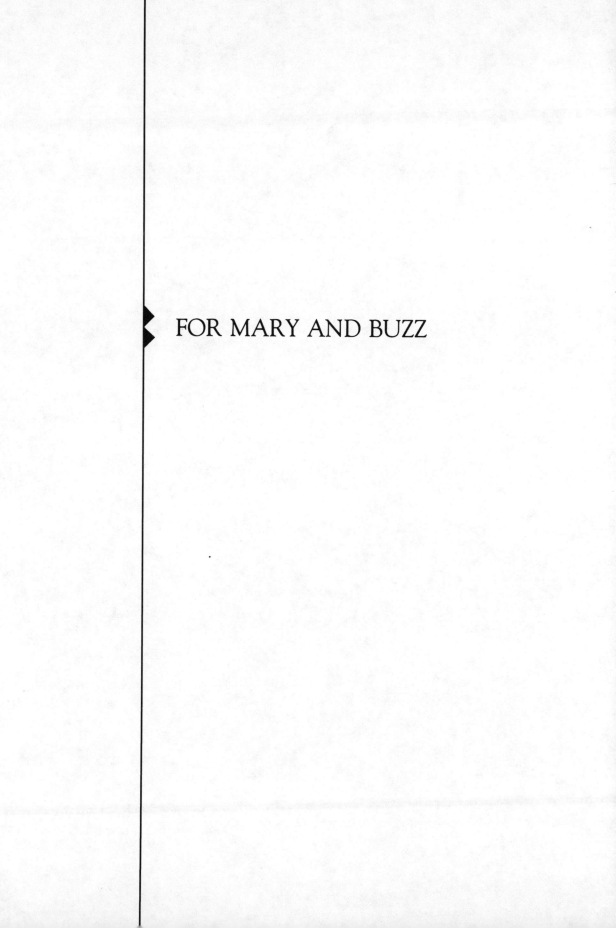

FOR MARY AND BUZZ

ONE MUST LEARN
BY DOING THE THING; FOR THOUGH YOU
THINK YOU KNOW IT
YOU HAVE NO CERTAINTY, UNTIL YOU TRY.

SOPHOCLES

CONTENTS

ACKNOWLEDGMENTS

TOM NEWKIRK SUGGESTED TO PHILIPPA STRATTON THAT HEINEMANN consider gathering a volume of my essays; I am grateful to him and to Philippa for taking up his suggestion. I am also thankful for the teachers across the United States and Canada whose questions and stories about their classrooms have continued to push my thinking about literacy instruction, and for the friends who respond to my writing in ways that keep me writing—Mary Ellen Giacobbe, Donald Graves, Toby McLeod, Donna Maxim, Donald Murray, Tom Newkirk, Katherine Stiles, and Susan Stires.

I am especially indebted to Dixie Goswami of the Bread Loaf School of English and to the trustees of Mr. Bingham's Trust for Charity for their encouragement and generous support.

In addition, thanks to Donna Bouvier, Manager of Editing and Production at Heinemann; to the teachers and the children and their parents for permission to reproduce material not previously published; and to the following for previously published material:

Chapter 2, pp. 34–35: "A Time to Talk" from *The Poetry of Robert Frost* edited by Edward Connery Lathem. Copyright 1916, 1923, © 1969 by Holt, Rinehart and Winston. Copyright 1944, 1951 by Robert Frost. Reprinted by permission of Henry Holt and Company, Inc.

Chapter 5, pp. 81–82: "You Can't Write a Poem About McDonald's" reprinted from *Tunes for Bears to Dance To,* by Ronald Wallace, by permission of the University of Pittsburgh Press. © 1983 by Ronald Wallace. Reprinted by permission of the publisher.

Chapter 5, pp. 82–83: "Maybe Dats Youwr Pwoblem Too" reprinted from Jim Hall, *The Mating Reflex* by permission of Carnegie Mellon University Press. © 1980 by Jim Hall.

Chapter 5, p. 83: "Stars" from *Spin a Soft Black Song* by Nikki Giovanni. Copyright © 1971, 1985 by Nikki Giovanni. Reprinted by permission of Farrar, Straus and Giroux, Inc.

Chapter 5, pp. 83–84: "While I Slept" reprinted from *Robert Francis: Collected Poems, 1936–1976* (Amherst: University of Massachusetts Press, 1976), copyright © 1936, 1964 by Robert Francis. Reprinted by permission of the publisher.

Chapter 5, p. 84: "Child Frightened by a Thunderstorm" reprinted by permission of the author, Ted Kooser.

Chapter 5, p. 84: "The Mill Back Home" reprinted from Vern Rutsala, *Walking Home from the Ice House* by permission of Carnegie Mellon University Press. © 1981 by Vern Rusala. Reprinted by permission of the publisher.

Chapter 5, p. 85: "Stone" from *Dismanteling the Silence* by Charles Simic. Copyright © 1971 by Charles Simic. Reprinted by permission of George Braziller, Inc.

Chapter 5, pp. 85–86: "The Puzzle" by Dennis Lee, from *Jelly Belly,* published by Macmillan of Canada, © Dennis Lee. Reprinted by permission.

Chapter 5, pp. 86–87: "Incident" reprinted by permission of GRM Associates, Inc., Agents for the Estate of Ida M. Cullen. From the book *On These I Stand* by Countee Cullen. Copyright © 1925 by Harper & Brothers; copyright renewed 1953 by Ida M. Cullen.

Chapter 5, p. 87: "What's That Smell in the Kitchen?" from *Circles on the Water* by Marge Piercy. Copyright © 1982 by Marge Piercy. Reprinted by permission of Alfred A. Knopf, Inc.

Chapter 5, p. 88: "My Favorite Word " from Lucia and James Hymes, Jr., *Ooodles of Noodles,* © 1964 by Addison Wesley Publishing Co., Inc., Reading, Massachusetts. Reprinted with permission of the publisher.

Chapter 5, pp. 92–93: "Sort of a Sestina" by Bruce Bennett. Reprinted by permission of the author.

Chapter 5, pp. 98: "Stopping by Woods on a Snowy Evening" from *The Poetry of Robert Frost* edited by Edward Connery Lathem. Copyright 1916, 1923, © 1969 by Holt, Rinehart and Winston. Copyright 1944, 1951 by Robert Frost. Reprinted by permission of Henry Holt and Company, Inc.

Chapter 7, p. 119: "Here Are My Hands" from *Here Are My Hands* by Bill Martin, Jr. New York: Henry Holt, 1987. Reprinted by permission of the author.

INTRODUCTION

THE FIRST TIME I READ DONALD GRAVES'S FOREWORD TO *IN THE Middle*, his declaration that "Atwell has no method" gave me pause. Since I had looked at *In the Middle* as three hundred pages of method, I was interested to know what he thought was going on here. Graves went on to describe my teaching as "a full-immersion approach to reading and writing, an immersion not unlike the acquisition of a new language, where only the new language can be spoken." I had to rethink method.

It's true that my experience of literacy and teaching had led me to develop systems for evaluating, keeping records, conferring, organizing the classroom, and so on. But as my experience grew more diverse and more complex, it was less and less mediated by traditional views of method, of a teacher who's up there orchestrating a program. When I wrote, read, and discovered what I and others did as writers and readers, I began to recognize the conditions that fostered engagement and excellence. Eventually I gained enough confidence in my own literacy to start behaving like a speaker of the new language that Graves described and to invite—and then to *expect*—my students to speak it with me. Because it was such a rich, compelling, and useful language, we tried to speak it all of the time, and we discovered what was possible for us as writers and readers in a public school classroom. Best of all, it was a language we could speak outside of the classroom, whenever people are engaged in authentic acts of writing and reading.

Side by Side explores some corners of the new language. Although the eight chapters address a variety of topics, from special education and critical thinking to reader response theory, poetry, and beginning literacy, two threads run through them. Each essay challenges programs that distance teachers from students and distort the processes we hope they will learn. And each urges teachers to become more active both in the classroom and out of it, to move beyond method and to sit side by side with students as observers of learning and participants in writing and reading.

The first chapter, "The Thoughtful Practitioner," is about my experience as a teacher-researcher and what the term has come to mean to me. I worry about attempts to package teacher-research as another formula to be followed, shutting down the possibility of surprise through a slavish adherence to the conventions of experimental inquiry. For me the point of the teacher-research movement is the intense satisfaction to be found in learning as a member of a scholarly community that begins in the classroom and extends beyond it to a literate engagement with the world. Its power lies not in establishing tight controls to prove an instructional bias, but in thinking side by side with others—our students among them—who care as much about writing, literature, and learning as we do.

In the scholarly community of my classroom in Boothbay Harbor, eighth graders were grouped heterogeneously for writing and reading, including students from the junior high resource room. "A Special Writer at Work" tells about one of these students, Laura, and what I learned from her about school environments that move remedial students into the mainstream. The new language of the workshop was especially relevant to the Lauras. While my other students were making the transition from traditional language arts methods, Laura was recovering from years of structured linguistic programs—language fractured into its tiniest and most trivial pieces, drilled and tested so that the very students who needed the most sense from literacy instruction got the least. The language that she heard spoken by me, her more able classmates, and the authors she read was music to her ears. Suddenly, writing and reading were good for something.

Chapter 3 explores a new wrinkle in drill-and-skill approaches: critical thinking programs. The same publishers who so successfully decontextualized writing and reading have begun to work their special magic on cognition. Because programmed instruction across the curriculum has traditionally bypassed critical thinking by emphasizing discrete skills and memorization, publishers have invented a new genre to remedy a situation that they helped to create, and schools seem to be eating it up. Teachers whose classrooms function as workshops recognize that in the course of a year's immersion in writing and reading, critical thinking becomes a natural, integral part of the curriculum. When writing and reading—and math, science, and history—are good for something, thinking happens, and it is good for something, too.

"When Readers Respond" is a consideration of literature-based reading programs. This is an exciting time to be a reading teacher. More and more teachers, from kindergarten through high school, are discovering the literature available to their students and shelving basals and anthologies in favor of classroom libraries of trade books—with varying degrees of success. Often, in spite of the best of intentions, our imaginations remain in the grip of the programs we put aside. It's difficult to immerse ourselves or our students in literature when our heads are full of reading skills invented for teacher's manuals, when our goal is to ensure that students read what they are supposed to read and "get" what they are supposed to "get." I have found Louise Rosenblatt's transactional theory to be of particular help as I examine the questions I ask young readers, respond to their responses, and come to terms with the reasons that I'm teaching with literature in the first place, including the importance of literature in my own life and the effects of my literacy on the lives of my students.

I met a teacher recently who sells encyclopedias as a summer job. He commented that some of his customers have never owned a book. I replied that encyclopedias were among the few books in my house when I was growing up. They represented a major financial investment for my family, and my brother and I read every volume many times, from cover to cover as if they were novels. The teacher remarked in surprise, "I guess I assumed that your parents were English teachers, from the way you talk about literature."

As parents, there may be no greater gift we can give our children than a literate household to grow up in. But as teachers, we have to work from the premise that all students, no matter their household, will read and will talk about literature as if it's their daily bread. In my life I had just two teachers who invited me to become a reader. Two were enough.

In sixth grade, Jack Edwards read to us long after his colleagues had abandoned such "childish" activities as read-alouds. He loved novels, and through him I met Beverly Cleary and E. B. White. It is Mr. Edwards's voice that I hear when I read *Charlotte's Web* to my daughter at bedtime, and I try to make my voice as joyful as his was.

The other teacher is my husband. I have written about our dining-room table, this literate environment where we argue, joke, and gossip about what we are reading. I know that some part of my passion for books comes from my admiration of Toby and from wanting to be like him, and I think of this often when I am teaching. Do our students, as readers, wish to be like us?

Other than the agony of round robin reading in the primary grades, I recall almost nothing else about how I was taught reading and literature. Although somewhere along the line I did learn to read, I do not remember or celebrate the teachers who followed the curriculum, teaching the requisite skills in the basal, as I do those who helped me to *become a reader.* Will our students remember us as the teachers who helped them *become readers?*

My husband was also the teacher who invited me to be a reader of poems. The distillation of language in poetry makes it at once the loveliest genre and the most powerful. Sadly, it is also the genre least taught in our schools and most likely to be reduced to a formula when it is. Poetry intimidates and mystifies teachers who were themselves mystified and intimidated in high school and undergraduate lit courses. Chapter 5, "Finding Poetry Everywhere," is an invitation to teachers to discover what poetry really does, bring it into their lives, and share it with their students.

Chapter 6 began as a speech. I was asked to join a panel at an NCTE convention in addressing the topic "When Bad Things Happen to Good Ideas." By then I had seen enough bad things happen to *In the Middle* to have a sense of its faults, among them the temptation to view the workshop as a method and simply borrow its trappings. But I have also visited and read about exemplary classrooms at all levels and in every kind of community where students read and write as avidly and thoughtfully as my eighth graders did. "When Writing Workshop Works" considers the characteristics of teachers whose classrooms invite immersion in writing and reading. I believe that the teachers' literacy is the key. In their classrooms there is little that Graves would describe as method and much diversity, purpose, and passion as teachers borrow the structure of the workshop in order to develop and share their own expertise as writers and readers.

The essay in this collection closest to my heart is about my daughter, Anne. Although her birth is one reason that I left the classroom, I have had no regrets—among other reasons, because of the ways that my eighth graders prepared me to be her parent. What I learned sitting side by side with them became a prism for looking at the beginnings of Anne's literacy. Just as in the classroom, because I was looking, I saw; and because I created ways to capture experiences, I remembered them and learned from the patterns that emerged over time. "Bringing It All Back Home" is about the happy parallels between the literate behaviors of adolescents and those of a toddler and between the roles an adult plays as teacher, researcher, writer, reader, and parent in creating conditions for literacy and forging literary apprenticeships with children of every age.

Side by Side concludes with a reconsideration of *In the Middle*. Since the latter was published I have received over a thousand letters from teachers. There can never be a second edition of *In the Middle*—it is the story of a particular time and place. But teachers' responses and my second thoughts prompted an essay about answers to the most frequent questions—about dialogue journals, conferences, discipline, working with low-tracked groupings, and stretching a given syllabus—as well as about things that I would change about the book if I were writing it today. It was a pleasure to step back inside the world of *In the Middle* through the stories that teachers shared in their letters. And it was an inspiration to know of so many teachers engaged side by side with students and colleagues in work that is real.

One recent Sunday afternoon Eben stopped by our house. In 1980 he was a student in my first writing workshop at Boothbay Region Elementary School. We sat at the table in the sunshine, reminiscing about eighth grade and talking about what he is reading—Hermann Hesse, Ken Kesey, Kurt Vonnegut. Before he left he borrowed Michael Ondaatje's *In the Skin of the Lion*, and after he was gone I washed out our coffee cups and remembered a line from Vonnegut's *Slapstick*. In the novel, Wilbur Daffodil-11 Swain becomes President of the United States on the strength of a pledge to provide every citizen with thousands of artificial relatives. His campaign slogan is "Lonesome no more!"

Every day I sat side by side in my classroom with students who spoke my language; some of them, like Eben, grew up to be adults who continue to speak it. For me one of the worst things about teaching a method or a program is the loneliness: I will never forget what it was like to stand there by myself at the front of the room, delivering directions and holding forth about topics that did not matter to me and did not make sense to my students. One of the best things about immersing ourselves and our kids in writing and reading is that teaching is lonesome no more.

1 THE THOUGHTFUL PRACTITIONER

I WAS GRATEFUL WHEN REXFORD BROWN REJECTED THE DREAD PHRASE "critical thinking skills" (1987). Instead, he considered how a school might reward or discourage *thoughtfulness*, a word that suggests human characteristics far more complex and desirable than any of the current jargon. He asks, "Can schools as we know them become more thoughtful places and produce students who are themselves more thoughtful?" (50)

Yes. The answer is yes—when teachers in a school are allowed and encouraged to be *thoughtful practitioners*. When teachers ask questions about students' learning, observe in their classrooms, and make sense of their observations, schools become more thoughtful places. When teachers change in light of their discoveries, when their teaching becomes more patient, more responsive, and more useful to students, schools become more thoughtful places. When teachers invite students to become partners in inquiry, to collaborate with them in wondering about what and how students are learning, schools become more thoughtful places. And when teachers act as scholars, closely reading, heatedly debating, and generously attributing the published work in their field, schools become more thoughtful places. In short, the most thoughtful practitioner is the teacher who acts as a researcher.

In this essay I'll explore four kinds of thoughtfulness that characterize the work of teacher-researchers, and I'll juxtapose thoughtfulness with what I know to be its nemesis: ignorance. According to Frank Smith,

3

Ignorance is not a matter of not knowing, but of not knowing that you don't know or mistakenly believing that you do know or that at least some expert somewhere does know. Ignorance is not so much not knowing an answer as not knowing that there is a question. . . . Ignorance is a blind dependence that someone else will be able to tell you what to do. (1983, 1)

I spent my first six years in the classroom looking for the someone elses who would tell me what to do. I read about the methods of Moffett, Tchudi, and Elbow and applied them liberally to my kids. When the method didn't work, or didn't work with everyone, I blamed Moffett, Tchudi, and Elbow. Worse, I blamed my kids. Then I looked around for some new gurus, some new systems and recipes; my only consolation is that I didn't look to commercial programs and an industry fueled by teacher ignorance. In truth, I didn't know what writers and readers actually do when they use language to make meaning, and I didn't know the individual writers and readers in my classroom because I was so busy orchestrating whole-class methods.

The work of one researcher changed all of this for me. Donald Graves published the results of his study at Atkinson Academy (1983), and everywhere teachers came out from behind our big desks and hodge-podge programs in order to move among our students, follow their leads, observe their learning, ask them genuine questions, and revise and revise our behavior as teachers. The day that I filed away my last program and invited eighth graders to develop their own topics, purposes, audiences, and processes was the birthday of thoughtfulness in my classroom. It was probably the first occasion when I had thought critically about my own teaching. This is one definition of thoughtfulness that I want to consider: the careful way that teacher-researchers continually examine and analyze their teaching. What happened in my classroom changed because suddenly I was observing what was going on there.

One of the most conspicuous changes in my teaching was in my methods for grading student writing. Instead of regarding evaluation as a system of rewards and punishments, I learned to view it as an opportunity for research. At the end of each quarter I conferred with individuals about their uses and views of writing, documented and analyzed what they said, set goals with them for the next nine weeks, and set a grade on their progress toward the goals of the previous quarter. One November, during our first round of evaluation conferences, I made an occasion for students to articulate the themes of the opening months of writing work-shop by asking, among other things, "What's the most important or useful thing you've learned as a writer in the first quarter?" Figure 1–1 shows one student's response, by way of example.

In mini-lessons that autumn I had stressed leads and conclu-sions, self-editing and proofreading, and a writer's need to be his or her own first critic. I assumed that my students would give back what I had given them, so that I could begin to formalize a sequence of mini-lessons for the eighth grade. Instead, the twenty-three students in just one of my classes named almost forty different kinds of knowledge, from new conventions to new techniques to new habits:

FIRST QUARTER EVALUATION CONFERENCE RESPONSES:
NOVEMBER

RESEARCH QUESTION:

What's the most important or useful thing you've learned as a writer in the first quarter?

NEW CONVENTIONS

Putting more paragraphs in and indenting more to show
    paragraphs
How to use the two left-hand margins
To use the skills on my skills list, especially how to use
    quotation marks
Headings and sub-headings: using these as ways to orga-
    nize my pieces
A comma can't hold two sentences together. I always
    thought it would (2)
Putting periods where my voice drops and stops
Ellipses to show a long pause
How to set up a business letter
How to set up my penpal letters and where to put my
    address and name
The colon rules
Their/they're/there
Homonyms

Circling words I'm not sure of and looking up their spellings

To keep my own list of spelling words that I can look at in my folder

NEW TECHNIQUES

Trying new things like flashbacks and embedding context. I was afraid to try stuff like that before, afraid I'd flub up really bad

To delete—to take things out that I don't need in the piece. Maybe I'm just braver this year.

Metaphors. I like them. They're hard and they make you think about *how* you'll write.

Parody. I just love it. I'll probably do some more.

The "My Ideas for Writing" sheet. I really try to keep it up. I add things once in a while and go back and look at it when I get stuck.

Different kinds of leads—dialogue, action, reaction

To describe what I'm feeling, not tell just the facts (3)

To use conversation; I used to just write what happened

To give examples that show. Instead of saying, "Daren spoke very loudly," I wrote, "Daren's voice boomed as if it were coming at me through a megaphone."

NEW HABITS

Looking at my writing from a reader's point of view: I never did that before.

Writing about things I want to write about, not everyone on the same topic like in 6th grade

To take my time

To work on individual pieces more, rather than turning out a lot of pieces

I used to copy other people's ideas, like the poem about the red flower with the green stem, or write about the same topics over and over. Now I try to write about what I care about and think up as many topics of my own as I can.

You can't write everything personal and then put it out in public. Now I write maybe once a week in a diary that only I see.

FIGURE 1–1

One Student's Response

QUARTERLY EVALUATION CONFERENCE NOTES

NAME __Jenn_____ QUARTER __1____

DATE __11/4_____ GRADE __B____

- **What does someone have to do in order to be a good writer?**

  Work really hard. Work hard on editing, on having enough conferences and getting others' opinions. Work on putting it together so it makes sense (and know when it doesn't have to make sense: poems, etc.). Know when you need to plan (my mystery), when you don't (poem), and when you want to see where your first draft will take you.

- **Which is your best piece of this quarter?**

  My mystery, even though it's not finished.

- **What makes it the best?**

  Because I worked so hard on it. I've never written one before. I had to put it together, to figure out how it would come out.

- **What's the most important or useful thing you've learned as a writer in the first quarter?**

  To work on individual pcs. more, rather than writing a lot of pcs. like last yr.

  To delete — to take things out that I don't need in the pc. Maybe just braver this yr.

- **What are your goals for the next quarter? (What do you want to try to do as a writer?)**

  Finish my mystery and try to get it published.

  Take on some other genre and try to get it published — a poem? Essay?

I had to rethink my teaching again. There were so few common responses that I abandoned hope of ever establishing a neat curriculum of mini-lessons. Whatever scope and sequence I developed would only limit what my students could do. And because there were so few common responses I became leery of ever talking about what eighth graders are like as writers. Within any grade level different students will make different errors and different discoveries, a fact that showed up most powerfully in Applebee's recent analysis of NAEP writing samples, which showed that most whole group instruction in conventions is a waste of time for most of the students in the group (1987). On the verge of orthodoxy, I rediscovered idiosyncrasy. Because the routine task of evaluation became a research task, I had opportunities at least every nine weeks to be thoughtful about my teaching.

As teacher-researchers we also have the opportunity to serve as models of thoughtfulness for our students. It was important when I read with eighth graders for them to see an adult joyfully obsessed with literature. And it was important when I wrote with them, not writing for its own sake but demonstrating how writing changes my life. But I am convinced that if my students remember me it will be as an adult who learned in public: as a researcher.

Rexford Brown writes, "The best way to restore balance to a system that is too heavily tilted toward the basics would be to create a strong counterculture within the system that values inquiry and thoughtfulness above all else" (1987, 52). This counterculture flourishes in the classrooms of teacher-researchers as we constantly demonstrate thoughtfulness and ask students to collaborate with us as partners in inquiry. Teacher-research is not a secret we keep from students for fear of skewing our findings. It is a model for our students of how adults can function as lifelong learners and of learning as a social activity.

When my students began developing their own ideas for writing, I was intrigued by the range of topics they chose. In evaluation conferences I asked, "Where do your ideas for writing come from?" They couldn't tell me, except in the most general terms. When I went back to my classes and asked, "Why couldn't you answer this question?" they responded, "It was too general. It's like asking someone, 'How do you decide what you'll eat?' It's different for different meals just like it is for different pieces of writing." Nine weeks later I asked, "Which is your best piece of

---

> **FIGURE 1–2** ◀

Sources of Ideas for Best Pieces of Writing

A regular schedule for writing, which leads students to think about their writing when they're not writing

The availability of a variety of materials: media are crucial in suggesting options

Conferences with others about their writing (peers and the teacher, and group share too)

Mini-lessons on genres, authors, and techniques

"Ideas for Writing" lists in daily folders

"Topics on Which I Have Written" lists in daily folders, and the writing stored in students' permanent folders

Discussions about where ideas for writing come from, making decisions about topic choice conscious

Discussions about where professional authors get their ideas

Whole-class topic searches during mini-lessons

Time for reading in class and readers' own choices of books, authors, and genres

Read-alouds by the teacher

Publication of student writing and calls for manuscripts for class magazines

Encouragement to write about science and social studies topics

Knowledge that the teacher allows writers to abandon pieces that aren't working or put them aside in favor of new ideas

The teacher's expectation that everyone will write

The teacher's interest in what everyone has to say

---

writing of this past quarter? How did you get the idea for *this piece?*" Now they could tell me—rich, specific anecdotes about how writing is born.

Three students volunteered to help me look at the results. We made up our own categories, putting the seventy-six responses into piles, sorting and re-sorting until we could name the variety of conditions that enabled writers to develop their own topics. Figure 1–2 shows the categories we developed that afternoon. This simple study taught me what teachers might think about in creating a writer's environment. The data informed my first published piece of research (1985); it also sparked a new trend in the classroom of writers talking about the sources of their ideas.

Although I left my classroom at Boothbay Region Elementary School three years ago, I'm just writing up the final piece of research that my students and I conducted together. Many of the kids in my last group had been writing since the third grade, and a collaborative inquiry afforded them a moment in time to stand back, contemplate, and celebrate their histories as writers. I asked each student, "What's the best thing that's ever happened to you as a writer?"

Figure 1–3 shows my recording of Mike's response. One reason I write while students talk, rather than tape-recording the evaluation conferences, is to slow down the interview. It gives them time to think about their responses, and it gives me time to respond to their responses. (A third factor was my discovery that it took me twelve hours to transcribe one hour of tape.) Mike started to tell me that the highlight of his writing career was in sixth grade when he won an essay contest, but that wasn't true. My transcription gave him time to change his mind.

After the class had shared their stories with each other, four students and I sorted, re-sorted, and then characterized the responses. In the process we identified the kinds of experiences that had made writing in school worthwhile by helping them to understand what writing is good for.

Many of my students said that others' responses to their writing were benchmarks in gaining a sense of themselves as writers. A special education student who was mainstreamed into my classroom remembered a time when I had shown a piece of her writing to the class on an overhead transparency, to demonstrate how writers can reveal character through dialogue. She explained, "No one had ever read one of my pieces to the class as an example of good writing." Another girl told about how her mother and grandfather wept in response to a poem she had written about the death of her grandmother. "It's not like I wanted to make them sad," she said, "but we could all be sad together. It helped." And one writer remembered her letter to *Kind* magazine, protesting laboratory experiments on animals, and the conversations it inspired. He commented, "Some people changed their minds because of what I wrote." These students could answer one of the most important questions about any

---

FIGURE 1–3

Mike's Response

QUARTERLY EVALUATION CONFERENCE NOTES

NAME *Mike*   **QUARTER** 3

GRADE B+

You've been writing now for a long time — perhaps as long as since third grade. What's the best thing that's ever happened to you as a writer?

> ~~In sixth grade when I won the Land Trust essay con~~
> I liked writing with Danny. It's just a whole different kind of writing — more fun and creative. We have a lot of laughs. We fit well together. We're sort of diff. — he jokes more and I'm more serious. But at times he can be serious too. Complement each other. First time I ever collaborated.

piece of writing—"Who is it for?"—because their teachers had worked hard at bringing real audiences for their writing into the classroom and made the unnatural seem natural.

Other students described collaborative projects with classmates as favorite memories. Two girls had written and performed a play in fifth grade, and two boys collaborated on a parody as eighth graders. They revealed something that I had forgotten as a teacher of writing: the power of two minds at play together. For the remainder of that school year I invited all the writers in my classes to develop and share ways that they could join forces on projects when collaboration suited their purposes.

Still other eighth graders described personal milestones in their writing careers and included the completion of major pieces of writing (a three-act play and a novel) as well as attempts to master new genres (essays and free verse poetry). One boy wrote, "In fifth grade I remember I tried two new things in one week. I used dialogue in a story, and I wrote a poem. Ever since that week, I felt confident about myself as a writer." Another writer referred to a journal entry that she had written in my classroom about an ordeal that had devastated her family: "When I wrote about the tragedy, it was like I got it out of my mind and onto the paper. After that, I didn't have to think about it any more."

These responses helped me understand how idiosyncratic writing can be and how important it is for individual students to be able to make significant decisions about their writing. Permitting my students to spend months of class time on such extensive projects as a novel and a play, trusting them to cope with difficulty, was a major step for me as a teacher; in the end, these difficult writing experiences were the ones that had meant the most to the writers. But at the same time that I allowed students to make decisions about their writing, I also provided direction by nudging individual kids, hard, to branch out and try unfamiliar genres, and by encouraging students with painful personal situations to write as a way to get some control over their responses. Instead of envisioning a scope and sequence of eighth-grade writing skills, I recognized a model of curriculum design that begins to account for the complexity of human needs.

Only two of my students mentioned positive evaluations as highpoints of their experiences as writers. One boy remembered the day the state department of education reported the eighth-grade assessment results, when he learned that he had scored at the 91st percentile in writing. He explained, "It was the highest of all of my test scores, by a lot. It's like the governor said to me, 'You are a writer, kid.'" The sole student who characterized a high grade in English as his best memory was a boy who had transferred into my room from another school system.

Our findings gave me new respect for my eighth graders. With the one exception, they spoke and wrote as writers, not as kids in an English class. Their confidence and authority, and their interest in considering and sharing their histories as writers, were by-products of an approach to teaching that said to students, your ideas and experiences matter. When teachers conduct research in our classrooms, we learn that kids' knowledge counts—and the kids do, too.

Frank Smith observes that "if thinking or asking questions seemed to pay off, and if some good models were around, children might even spend a few years at school doing just that—thinking and asking questions" (1983, 9). We know that children learn by example and by making sense of meaningful situations. Think of the example we set as teachers who conduct research, of the payoff when we make learning make sense, of the model we provide when we demonstrate curiosity and thoughtfulness. If we want to eradicate ignorance, I can't think of a better way to start than by showing our kids how we find the problems that interest us, in hope that they will find the problems that interest them.

Another way that we demonstrate thoughtfulness as teacher-researchers is through our concern with our colleagues, both within our schools and beyond. Teacher-research informs not only individual teachers and their students, but also the educators who read scholarly publications and attend professional conferences. As thoughtful practitioners we assume responsibility for the most difficult thinking of all: writing. But we are also thoughtful in the sense of having a selfless concern with the needs of others. We are considerate of what other teachers need to understand, of the kind of information that will help others rethink their teaching, and of the scholarly work already undertaken so that we don't keep replicating each other's work. We ask, "How can my research contribute to what is known?" Our answers, the contributions we make, are as varied and distinctive as our kids and classrooms. Three recent collections of teachers' research demonstrate the range.

In *Breaking Ground* (Hansen, Newkirk, and Graves 1985), Kathy Matthews tells about first graders who successfully integrated writing across the curriculum. Jack Wilde describes his fifth graders' growth as authors of fiction and his role in encouraging students to "incorporate play and power in the service of plausibility" (131). Linda Rief recounts the experiences of eighth graders who gathered information from primary sources by interviewing their grandparents and residents of a local nursing home.

In *Seeing for Ourselves* (Bissex and Bullock 1987), Alice DeLana observes the development of three high school students as they respond in writing to her art history course. Elizabeth Cornell describes the effects of the regular reading of poetry on the writing and reading of her first graders. And Carol Avery traces a year in the life of Traci, a learning-disabled student in her whole language classroom.

In the second edition of *Understanding Writing* (Newkirk and Atwell 1988) Siusan Durst recounts the year that her first graders took turns caring for Oscar, a stuffed bear, and writing daily journal entries about his experiences that provide a crucial link between students' lives in and out of school. Anne Bingham and Tim Rynkofs demonstrate how they use writing folders to document student progress, and Ellen Blackburn Karelitz examines the neglected genre of note writing, both who wrote notes in her primary classroom and why. In the conclusion to her chapter Karelitz writes, "Teachers are continually inventing new solutions to old problems, but we must document our solutions for each other" (113). As thoughtful practitioners, teacher-researchers document out of consideration for those other teachers who know they don't know.

There is another sense in which the thoughtful practitioner is considerate. The published body of teachers' research has grown so enormous that it may be difficult to keep straight exactly who should receive credit for documenting a particular new solution to a particular old problem. But we have to try, out of respect for our colleagues everywhere and for the teacher-researcher movement itself.

Recently I reviewed a manuscript that described a primary teacher's attempts at connecting writing and reading in her classroom. The teacher administered a spelling test to her students to determine their knowledge of letter and word features. The test was familiar. Although no attribution was given, it was developed by Mary Ellen Giacobbe and reported in her article "Kids Can Write the First Week of School," one of the first published pieces of teacher-research (1981). The data transformed many primary teachers' approaches to writing and reading by helping to dispel the belief that children must learn to read before they are allowed to write in school. It also gave teachers of young writers a simple, revealing method to use in determining patterns among their students' spellings.

It is thrilling to Mary Ellen, to all of us, when others borrow from our research and from the methods we have documented. It is the reason we write and speak—so that teachers and their students may take advantage of the new solutions we invent in our classrooms. But as thoughtful practitioners I hope we can remember to be generous and to cite the classroom teachers whose work influences our own, to proudly align ourselves with a community of teachers just as we are proud to align ourselves with university researchers.

There is one more kind of thoughtfulness that characterizes the work of teacher-researchers; I'll call it scholarship. Rexford Brown writes, "Thoughtfulness requires close reading and disciplined debate about what has been read" (1987, 51). Teacher-researchers are probably the ideal consumers of educational research because we are also its producers. We look for application of research to practice as well as to our own studies. We look at the products of others' research, but we also look at their processes as researchers. And we especially look at the process-observational research of the last decade, at the work of Glenda Bissex, Lucy Calkins, Marie Clay, Janet Emig, Yetta and Ken Goodman, Donald Graves, Shirley Heath, Thomas Newkirk, Sondra Perl, Mina Shaughnessy, Nancy Sommers, Susan Sowers, Denny Taylor, and Nancy Wilson. When researchers such as these explain and explore context, we understand why teachers and learners are teaching and learning. When researchers such as these develop theories based on their close descriptions of behavior in context, we understand how we might build the theories that inform our practice. Perhaps more than any other educational researchers we need to hold ourselves to rigorous, high standards, to read and relate our work to the various fields that inform our research: composition and literacy studies, but also rhetorical studies, linguistics, literary criticism, psychology, anthropology; to read and consider Howard Gardner, L. S. Vygotsky, Robert Coles, Paulo Freire, I. A. Richards, Eudora Welty, Clifford Geertz, Vera John-Steiner, Seymour Papert, Louise Rosenblatt, Eliot Eisner, William Stafford, John Gardner. Frank Smith writes:

> The opposite of ignorance is keeping the mind alive, always considering alternatives, never shutting the system down. It is remembering that every question might be put differently, that authority is not necessarily right, and that superficial glibness . . . is not necessarily erudition. The opposite of ignorance is never to rest content doing something you do not understand. (1983, 9)

I worry that the debate over whether a classroom teacher can ever really be a real researcher may find its roots in work by and about teacher-researchers that is less than contemplative. There is a danger that we could rest content doing something we do not understand. As we continue to consider what teacher-research is, we should be aware that it is not theory-stripped, context-stripped method-testing. We need to reject impoverished models that turn classroom inquiry into a pseudoscientific horse race. One way we do this is by learning from the best research reports and by recognizing that close reading and disciplined debate about what we have read will strengthen, not dilute, our power as thoughtful practitioners.

When I reached this point in drafting this essay, I read what I had written so far to my husband and asked him how he thought I should end it. He suggested, "Let us pray."

Instead, I'll conclude by sharing another conversation we have had recently, this time about our daughter, who is a few years away from starting school. We asked each other, "What do you want from school for Anne?"

At our house, we dream big.

We hope for a teacher who will understand writing, reading, and Anne: someone who will observe what she knows and needs to know next, how she learns, and what she loves, someone who will speak to us of our daughter's literacy with passion and insight, someone so thoughtful about teaching and learning that when we visit Anne's classroom there isn't a program in sight. We dream of the thoughtful practices of a teacher-researcher.

I have long believed that teachers of reading and writing were special. Now, as a parent, I agree with Frank Smith: reading and writing are the most important things in the world; therefore, teachers of reading and writing are the most important people in the world. But the thoughtful practitioner is the best of the most important people in the world.

2
A SPECIAL WRITER AT WORK

What the child can do in cooperation today he can do alone tomorrow. Therefore the only good kind of instruction is that which marches ahead of development and leads it; it must be aimed not so much at the ripe as the ripening function.

L. S. Vygotsky

I N OUR TEACHING OF WRITING AND OUR COMPOSITION SCHOLARSHIP, we often tap Vygotsky when considering the transactions we conduct with young writers. We ask, how can writing instruction march ahead of development and lead it? The literature of the profession is filled with our answers—stories of students and teachers who discover in cooperation what children can do, case studies rich with the context of the classroom that show mediated learning and all its flowers.

Laura, an eighth-grade writer, brought me back to Vygotsky after a spell when I thought I had learned all the lessons that he might have to teach me. Laura cooperated in varied and subtle ways with many teachers: me, her friends and the other kids in her class, Judy Blume, and Robert Frost. Our teaching wasn't aimed at the ripe—what Laura already was—but at the ripening function. Laura was already a special education student; she became an accomplished writer and reader. Laura overcame her classification. Mainstreaming her into a writing and reading workshop, where she was one of twenty-five eighth graders of every ability, allowed Laura to reach far beyond the limits her school had set for her.

For a long time I had looked upon Boothbay's special ed students as walking packages of clinically defined disabilities. Batteries of tests administered by the school psychologists produced technical diagnoses I would not have dreamed of challenging—let alone reading. I didn't have to. Although I was the eighth-grade English teacher, eighth graders identified by the tests as language disabled did not come to me for English.

They were tracked into the reading lab and the junior high resource room. There I assumed they received scientific instruction designed to remedy their particular disabilities. Each year I ignored the ghosts in my school, the eight or ten eighth graders who never came to my room.

I carried on in this complacent way until Susan Stires, one of Boothbay's special education teachers, began to question the batteries of tests, the various "scientific" labels, and the prescribed remedial work. She showed me how remediation in language arts most often addresses skills in isolation—handwriting, spelling, verb forms, sequencing, sentence structure, paragraph organization, and so on. Students complete endless exercises in their identified areas of weakness, mountains of worksheets and workbook pages designed by the same people who design the tests. Students seldom write anything beyond single sentences. They rarely read real books. The "structured, individualized, linguistic approach" defines the ripening function as the next skill in the sequence invented by the test manufacturer, under the assumption that students will only be remediated when enough isolated skills are divided and conquered. It is hardly surprising that few are remediated. Exercises do little to inspire commitment or excellence and nothing to suggest the power and satisfaction of full-blown literacy.

Susan was the only special education teacher in a group of Boothbay Elementary faculty who began working together in 1980 to develop a writing program for our K–8 students. She joined the project because she had the insight and compassion to look beyond the folders of test results to see individual children. Some were truly language disabled, some were temporarily disabled by the curriculum or home situations, all of them were interesting, interested human beings with something to say. Susan put away the kits and dittoes, gave her resource room students paper, and transformed her language program into a writers' workshop.

Like the kids of the other teachers in the project, Susan's students wrote every day. They chose their own subjects and genres. They conferred about the content of their writing. They published what they wrote, and their voices were heard throughout our school. Susan learned to teach in the context of pieces of writing, to help with those parts of the process with which children encountered difficulty, and to give her students all the time they needed to write well. She learned how to cooperate with them, encouraging, questioning, offering opinions and strategies. And she helped the rest of us, her colleagues, begin to penetrate the wall of jargon, assumption, and arrogance surrounding special education programs (Stires 1983 a and b).

Because of Susan's work I argued to have eighth-grade special education students placed in my classroom for English. By then my classroom, too, had become a writers' workshop, a place where individuals discovered and acted on their own intentions, not the teacher's single intention for a whole group. They took responsibility for developing topics and worked at their own pace. They received help one to one as I moved among writers conferring and as they conferred with each other. They represented in each class the whole range of grade-eight abilities, attitudes, and intentions. And it worked. There are twenty-five teachers in a workshop. Everyone learns from everybody, and less able students may learn most and best of all. Surrounded by more able models, learners whose ideas will spark and charge the environment, special education students have equal access to complex and worthwhile activities.

In the four years that learning disabled students were mainstreamed into my classroom, all of them succeeded. No one returned to the resource room. In many ways Laura's success was typical, just as she was typical of special students I have taught: shy and unsure of herself, a bit clingy, overweight and uncoordinated, less grown-up in her attitudes and tastes than the other eighth-grade girls, and out of the mainstream socially. But her success was special, too. From Laura I learned new meanings of Vygotsky's term "cooperation" because she took such full advantage of the resources that she found around her. Very little was wasted on Laura. Everything became grist for her literary mill.

Laura was first referred for testing at the beginning of second grade and identified then as language disabled. She had low-average abilities overall but real difficulty with memory, both short and long term. She couldn't memorize and retrieve factual information or retell what she was told. She became confused and lost her place when reading aloud. Her spelling was low as were her abilities to organize and sequence information.

Until eighth grade, Laura had half of her language arts instruction in the resource room. During the years that Susan Stires was her resource room teacher, Laura wrote. She spent the rest of her day, coming up through the grades, in a special class of low-tracked students who worked in various mastery programs. Laura was happy to be in a regular classroom in junior high. She said, "It's harder here, but at least it's not boring. We don't have to do those spelling cards. I like writing about things I want to write about, not everyone writing the same topic."

In eighth grade Laura wrote every day, just as everyone in her class did. I expected that she would. I also did as much as I could to make her writing possible. Although choosing her own topics was crucial to Laura, for her the hardest part of writing was topic choice. She became anxious whenever she finished one piece of writing and had to think about starting another. She did not want to be told what to write, but she did need help, and it came in many forms. Finding ideas for writing was the most obvious of the ways that she cooperated with me, other students, and the professional writers she read.

In reading workshop, a separate class from writing in which students selected their own books and read at their own pace, Laura chose Judy Blume. She was wild for Blume, ecstatic to be reading her novels in school, and absolutely impelled as a reader. Lucy Calkins has referred to the underground curriculum flourishing in our schools; for Laura, this meant Judy Blume. The following excerpts from Laura's reading journal were written during the first weeks of school.

September 9

Dear Ms. Atwell,

I am really getting into Judy Blume books. I like them because she doesn't write words or the book hard to read. She writes about mostly teenagers trying to grow up and to face problems. I like that because it helps me. Do know anyother authors who would make me interested in books like hers. Thanks.

9/18

Dear Ms. A.

Yes I have read those two books, there good. I finished then again maybe I want over the weekend. I read it of and on the diffrent day's. Now Im reading, "starring Sally J. As her self." By the one and only Judy Blume. This one is good but it say "Sally" all the time not like "I". I like it because it takes place in the time the war is over.

Sept 22.

Dear Mrs. Atwell,

Well I was looking over at your new books and guess what I found? I found "Deenie, by the one and only Judy Blume. All I have to do is finish *Starring Sally J. Freedman as herself* and the beginning of *Deenie* and I can go onto other authors and learn, and to be able to have adventures.

Sept 30

Dear Ms. Atwell,

I just finished *Deenie.* I just love her attitued about her brace, also how she and Buddy turned out to really like each other. I hope I get a response by Judy Blume, the letter I'm writing her. Do you think so?

How was the trip you took this weekend? In Mrs. Reeds Room, we were talking about you (not bad things). We were saying how we liked you and how you fly someplace and be back the next day, being pregnat too. That's all know. Bye!

The last letter described one of Laura's first pieces of writing of the school year; it also carried the germ of the idea for her next. She had written Blume a letter, the first she had written to someone she didn't know. The early drafts consisted of a single long paragraph. In an editing conference about the final draft we paragraphed it together by figuring out where Judy Blume's eyes could use some breaks. In the letter Laura is already writing like a writer, wanting to know to what extent Blume's novels are autobiographical, asking after Blume's plans, and commenting on her titles.

——— Street
Boothbay, Maine 04537

September 1

Judy Blume
c/o Dell Publishing Co., Inc.
1 Dag Hammarskjold Plaza
New York, New York 10017

Dear Ms. Blume:

I'm one of your greatest fans. I want you to know I have read all your books. I have two things to ask you.

First, are you part of the main character in your books? Second, do you plan to write more? I hope so.

The one book I liked was *It's Not the End of the World*. I liked it because my parents got a divorce, and it helped me learn about other people's feelings, even if it's not true.

I hope some day I would be able to meet you in person. One thing that got me interested in your books was your titles. That's all I have to say. It's been a pleasure having someone like you read this.

Sincerely,
Laura

Laura was also happy with me, at first because I let her read Judy Blume, but gradually because she discovered that sometimes I knew what I was talking about and she could make immediate use of what I shared. One way I shared was in mini-lessons, a technique developed by Lucy Calkins (1986). I took five minutes at the beginning of each day's workshop to present a quick lesson on an issue that I observed as relevant to some of the kids' writing.

Sometimes mini-lessons addressed classroom procedures and my expectations of writers in the workshop (for example, how to self-edit, confer with other students, prepare for evaluation conferences, keep records of proofreading skills and ideas for topics). Sometimes I discussed issues of craft and process (showing rather than telling, what makes a main character a main character, different genres and modes of writing, differences between recopying and revising). And on other days I talked about conventions and what readers expect of written texts (how to set up dialogue and business letters, when and how to paragraph, what various punctuation marks tell readers' eyes, how to keep verb tenses consistent).

Laura practically ate up any mini-lesson that suggested a possibility for a future piece of writing. She sat in the front group of desks, rapt with attention. In a procedural mini-lesson on writing resources available in the classroom I showed a folder of information about getting and keeping a pen pal. At the end of the week she gave me two dollar bills and asked if I would write a check for her to one of the pen-pal agencies; she had a letter ready to send. For the rest of the school year Laura corresponded regularly with Anna, an Irish thirteen-year-old, during writing workshop.

Another day's mini-lesson was a topic search, five minutes of talk about early memories of school, friends, and family. That morning Laura put away the piece she was working on and began a narrative about her first day of kindergarten at the old Boothbay Town Hall.

Laura also tapped reading workshop mini-lessons for her writing. When I read aloud examples of parody—from Woody Allen, Veronica Geng, and eighth graders—in order to introduce a new genre, Laura wrote a parody of the principal's newsletter to parents. I spent another week kicking off each reading workshop by sharing first pages from some of my favorite adolescent fiction. The day I read aloud from Robert Lipsyte's *One Fat Summer*, Laura added a "P. S. S." to a letter in her reading journal: "I just love the beginning of *One Fat Summer.*" A few days later she found a copy of the novel, her first departure of the school year from Judy Blume, and she loved the whole book. She wrote about the effects of my reading aloud.

Oct. 2

Dear Ms. Atwell,

I really like it when you read to us. Also when you read *About David* I watched you while you read us that, and I got fascinated by the way your face expressed to what you read. I also owe you thanks for helping me decide on what are good and bad books to read, at the beginning of the period. I am almost finished with *One Fat Summer. It's good!* I have read *fifteen* once a longtime ago, and I think I'll read a book that was enteresting and go back and read *fifteen* after. I was wondering, we can't write to you when you have your baby. Do we read and not write to you or are we having work to do? Got to go write in Kim's log.

Bye!

From
Laura

Laura was a sponge, soaking up everything. After years of programmed reading instruction, activities and exercises designed to remediate her poor memory and deficient oral reading, she was getting help that she saw she could use. And because she was Laura, she could acknowledge its usefulness. She was truly panicked in October, afraid my maternity leave would send her back to drill-and-skill work. (During the seven weeks that I was gone, students corresponded with each other about their reading.)

In a mini-lesson that month in writing workshop, kids received copies of a list of all the different kinds of writing that students at our school had produced since the inception of the writing project. It is a long list comprising many genres (Atwell 1987). They tucked it into their daily folders as a reference, one more place to look when planning writing. When Laura finished the story she was working on, she fished out the list and circled the kinds of writing she wanted to try. The first she tackled was an interview.

Laura came into my homeroom one morning to ask if she could interview me during break, the junior high version of recess. I said sure, and she arrived at the end of third period with a list of questions she had prepared during her first period writing workshop. She sat across from me at my desk and wrote while I talked. Laura's notes appear as Figure 2–1.

The next day in class Laura used her notes to write a draft of a feature story (Figure 2–2), then asked if she could have group share. It was the first time that she had brought a piece of writing to the whole-class meeting that ended each workshop. She asked the other kids in the circle to listen and then tell her what they

Laura's Interview Notes

Enterview~to Ms. Atwell —

LAURA draft
8A
Oct. 17

When were you Bom — Was born in Buffalo NEW YORK

② What did you do when you were Younger that enterested you to be a teacher — NEVer wonted to be onE, She didn't liKE teachers, She got into troublE in school. shE onE a Schoolership ~ — to colLAGE, She liKED her colAgE English class a lot.

~When did you~ what was your childhood liKE —

When did you get mAniED — In 1973.

was it hard to chooSE between relationship or~a teacher — to be Teachening was in thE family, her husband tought He was her teacher at University of Buffalo.

~How that you are expecting a child what would itslow down your writting —~

When did you become A teacher — In 1973

How long have you been a writer — since 1980, when thE writing program started. (....)

► FIGURE 2–2 ◄

Laura's Feature-Story Draft

Ms. Atwell.   1draft
                                                              Oct. 18

      MS. Atwell was born in BUFFALO NEW YORK.
When she was younger she never wonted to be a teacher,
She alway got into ~~some~~ trouble, ①She ~~got~~ won a scoolership to COllAGE.
Ms. Atwell liked her English Class alot, so she stayed half A
year longer and was a student teacher.
      Ms. Atwell met her husband, when he was a teacher
                          when she was a student in his class   Also she became
at University of Buffalo. They got married in 1973, ~~also became~~
   teacher the SAME YEAR   writer
a ~~teacher the same year~~ In 1980 she became A ~~teacher~~
when thE writing Program stArted. When I Asked her, "Whats it
like to travel Alone with out your Husband," she said it was
mostly pretty boring, Also hard work so she doesn't miss him
much. Even if he was with her she wouldn't see him.
      She has Published one book and one Comming out
next year. ③Her Plans for thE future is to Continuing writing
and be a teacher, Also to teach teachers and students. I Am
writing this on Ms. Atwell becausE she is funny and fastAnating
to have for a teacher.

wanted to know more about. They had three questions, which
Laura wrote down so she would remember them:

> What things did she do to get in trouble in school?
> What did she think about becoming a writer?
> Could you tell more about the turning point of when she
> became a writer?

Laura made a second appointment with me for the next day at break and asked her new questions. But in the following day's class she was stuck. She said, "Now, how do I put this stuff in?" I reminded her about a mini-lesson in which I had demonstrated how to use numbers and other symbols as a code for indicating where something should be added and told her, "What you have to do is read over the draft and figure out where each piece of this new information will best fit." It took her the rest of the period to organize her new material. She inserted numbers, read through the new version, erased and reinserted numbers, and reread. Then she edited, I edited, and she wrote a final. Laura published the interview in *The BRES Reporter,* the school literary magazine, which was started by two of Susan Stires's resource room students.

In backtracking through the piece, I think some amazing things happened given Laura's history. First, she asked for group share and read her piece aloud to the class in spite of her shyness and poor oral reading. She wanted the help that she had seen students in the group could provide. She knew from past experience that nothing bad would happen when she read, that kids would listen hard, tell back what they heard, and ask questions about things they wanted to know more about.

Next, organizing and classifying information were two of the problems consistently noted in Laura's psycho ed test results. Confronted with a real task—something she wanted to do, questions about which she was genuinely curious—she figured out how to organize herself. She prepared by writing down beforehand the questions she wanted to ask, and when I asked how she knew to do this she replied, "That's what they do on TV." Later, when she had trouble adding the answers to her new questions, she asked for a strategy and then discovered on her own how to use it.

Finally, Laura's most serious problem, as indicated by the testing, was a poor auditory memory: she had difficulty remembering what had been said. In the interview not only did Laura remember what I had said and write it down, she translated my words from first person to third person in her head as she wrote: each "I" became "she." The subject mattered to her, and she used resources she wasn't supposed to have to get it right.

In general, the skills identified in Laura's test results as deficiencies were not the areas she worked on in writing workshop in real pieces of her writing. In Figure 2–3, the list on the left is

---

FIGURE 2–3

Laura's Skills Lists

SAMPLE LANGUAGE SKILLS IDENTIFIED IN SPECIAL EDUCATION DIAGNOSES	SAMPLE LANGUAGE SKILLS IDENTIFIED IN PIECES OF LAURA'S WRITING
Grammar	Two left-hand margins, one for new paragraphs, on prose writing
Word endings	Circle any word that doesn't look right; then go back and look up its spelling
Verb endings	Will/well
Correct forms of present and past verb tenses	Won't/want
Synonyms	Were/where
Antonyms	Draft in paragraphs: guess and indent
Understanding and explaining idioms	Use ¶ when editing to indicate new paragraphs
Using descriptors of increasing quality/quantity	Three marks (, ? !) can go between a quote and its explanatory phrase; never a period
Understanding and creating analogies	Three-line heading on any letter
Arranging words in sentences in their logical order	Don't indent the greeting of a letter
Spelling	Comma after the closing of a letter
Classifyng	On a business letter, a colon after the greeting
Given an idea, creating a short story	No period at the end of a title
	A comma between a city and its state
	A *lot* is two words
	Capital letters on the first, last, and important words in a title
	A quote and its explanatory phrase usually belong in the same paragraph
	On a poem, indent the "leftovers"
	Listen for too many *as*'s or *when*'s at the beginning of sentences
	Apostrophe *s* to show something belongs to someone

---

drawn from her test results. The list on the right, from my conference journal, includes the skills I identified when editing pieces of Laura's writing and taught to her one at a time through the school year. She added them to the individual proofreading list stapled inside her daily writing folder and self-edited for each, as appropriate, on subsequent pieces of her writing. The only correspondence between the two lists is in the area of spelling, and even that is worded differently: in writing workshop we identified either specific word pairs or a general principle to help her spot and correct her misspellings.

Laura needed to learn many conventions; most of those on her list were not areas of weakness for her classmates. I don't believe that her specific problems with mechanics could have shown up in a commercial program—and even if they did, in what context? Surely not in a real letter to the beloved Judy Blume or a real story about Laura's grandmother's death or a real poem about Christa McAuliffe. When I asked in November what she had learned in the first nine weeks that she considered most important or useful she said, "Learning how to set up a pen-pal letter, where to put the addresses, and homonyms. I'm so glad you talked about them in mini-lessons because I think I know which one to use a lot of the time now." Laura didn't need more skills, taught in isolation in a structured, individualized, linguistic approach, before she was allowed to write. She needed to write and along the way learn the conventions that she didn't yet know by trying to put them to work for her.

Writing poetry without an assigned format was another accomplishment during Laura's year in eighth grade. I read poems aloud in mini-lessons—Robert Frost, Elizabeth Bishop, Shel Silverstein, Richard Wilbur, Valerie Worth, e e cummings, students in the class and previous years' classes—then made photocopies available so students could make individual anthologies and own their favorite poems. Laura collected a folder full of her favorites. In February, after the NASA shuttle disaster, she wrote her first free-verse poem. She said, "I really liked that Christa McAuliffe. I was upset and mixed up, and this is the way I expressed my feelings."

ALL WE KNOW

All we know is that she lived in a small town
    called Concord,
That she had a family,
And that she was a social studies teacher.
All we know is that she had a dream to go to space,
That her dream almost came true,
That she was going to teach class while in space,

> That she had a chance to explain to us about
>   our outer world,
> And that she took her son's teddybear to be
>   the first in space.
> All we know is that she and six others boarded
>   the shuttle with happiness and hope,
> That they had a good lift-off,
> That millions of people were watching the launch,
> And that they will never come back to tell us
>   about their discoveries.
> All we know is that seven moons will be named
>   after them.
> That the families agree that life must go on,
> And that they will be missed.
> All we hope is that they went in peace.

After I returned from maternity leave I read "All We Know" and talked with Laura about it. I asked, "Why 'All We Know'? How did you come up with the idea to use repetition?"

She said, "I remember some of the poems you read to us that had a lot of repeating. And on the day of the explosion they kept saying on TV, 'All we know at this time is blah, blah.' I kept hearing it, and I knew I wanted to use it." I asked her if she wanted to send a copy to the *Boothbay Register*, the local weekly, and she thought maybe. I said, "I'm thinking about that because there was a poem in the *Register* about the shuttle disaster by one of their reporters, and I think yours is—" She interrupted me. "Mine is better. I thought so, too."

This was the second time that Laura had used writing to help her come to grips with a highly charged emotional situation. The first, written in September, dealt with her grandmother's tragic death. She told me about how writing it had helped her. "When I try to talk about what happened, I get all nervous and upset. The words don't come out right. But when I write it down it's better. That piece is the best thing that ever happened to me as a writer. I was able to say what I thought. From then on I was able to express myself. I won't have to write about that ever again."

When teachers talk about students' writing as emotional catharsis, it makes me nervous, so I'm going to be careful here. I do think that some of Laura's oral language problems had an emotional basis. At times she was scattered and upset because of what she and her family had suffered. I did not hold her hand, counsel her, or urge her to write about her experiences. I did give her encouragement, space, time, and choice. Laura chose it, she got it out of her system by reflecting on and shaping it, and she went on. Although Laura's essay about her grandmother wasn't her best piece of writing by my standards, she identified it on three occasions during the school year as her best work. It was a hallmark for her. Later, when she was devastated by the *Challenger* disaster, she turned naturally to writing. And, again, she did more than emote. She used writing to control the situation: "All We Know" is a formal poem. Even as she watched the television that day and wept for McAuliffe, Laura's wheels were turning. She listened to Dan Rather's "all we know, all we know" and amidst her tears she thought, "I can *use* that."

Other students' writing also provided grist for Laura's mill. In a writing mini-lesson in the spring I announced an essay competition sponsored by Rotary Club International. Students were encouraged to write a letter to a world leader urging peace and specifying steps that could be taken to achieve it. Three students decided to enter, Laura among them. I dug out copies of essays that other eighth graders had written and showed different ways of approaching the task. Laura was taken with a Land Preservation Society essay by Luanne, which Luanne had introduced with the lyrics of a Pete Seeger song. She immediately started looking for a poem she could use in the same way in her letter to Mikhail Gorbachev. She started her first draft:

Laura
8A
1 draft
3/15

I pledge allegence to the flag of
the United States of America, and
to the republic for which it stands
One nation under god, indivible
with liberty and justice for all.

Dear Mr. Gobachowf,

Those are America's strong words, *with liberty and justice for all.* And thats why I write to you for peace.

After a day spent staring at this lead, Laura discovered it wasn't leading her anywhere remotely near world peace. She conferred with me, then began again by writing down all the things she could think of that might lead to a more peaceful world:

1 To be able to meet
   with ~~eachother~~ the President more often
   to here each other out for
   what they said to ~~each~~ one
   ~~other~~ another.
2 ~~To be able~~ to ~~no~~ have more
   kids exchange to one of our
   countrys to learn about our life
   and how it really isn't that different.
3 To foget the past and
   think of the present
4 ~~To let~~ to let the russians
   be able to come to America
   to live with there love one's
5 And to stop only war talks.

At my request she shared the list with Zandy and Teresa in a conference, and they asked questions about Laura's plan. She went back and elaborated on the list, then told me she was ready to write her essay but first she needed to find the right poem for her lead. She was determined to use a poem as Luanne had.

Laura spent the rest of the period, all of reading workshop, and almost two hours at home that night reading a Robert Frost collection, where she found "A Time to Talk," a poem about neighborliness. The next day she started her second draft, and over the following week and a half she wrote a third draft and then a final copy, which she submitted to the local Rotary Club. Laura's letter carried "A Time to Talk" as its epigraph and won second prize in the local contest.

A TIME TO TALK

When a friend calls to me from the road
And slows his horse to a meaning walk,
I don't stand still and look around

On all the hills I haven't hoed,
And shout from where I am, "What is it?"
No, not as there is a time to talk.
I thrust my hoe in the mellow ground,
Blade-end up and five feet tall,
And plod: I go up to the stone wall
For a friendly visit.

ROBERT FROST

Mikhail Gorbachev
The Kremlin
Moscow
The Soviet Union

Dear Mr. Gorbachev,

I also believe the Americans and Russians shall thrust their hoes in the mellow ground and meet soon at the stone wall, for a friendly visit.

For example, I wish you would meet with the President every year to hear each other out and to let us hear what was said between one another. I think it's important for us to be able to learn and share thoughts as one person, so there won't be any trouble or arguments over one topic. I also hope when you meet with the President you would address other topics, such as world hunger and sending more exports to needy countries.

Thirdly, I suggest that we exchange kids between our two countries, state to state, to learn about our lives and daily habits and to see how we the people are not different from one another.

I also wish you would let the families in Russia come to America to be with their loved ones, and that we could hold more programs a few times a year, by satellite, so we will have more contact with each other.

I would like to see the United States and the Soviet Union forget the past and think of the opportunities in the present.

Sincerely,
Laura

Laura sweated over the essay. She tried four new strategies in this one piece: brainstorming ideas, using a poem as an epigraph, cutting and pasting to reorder ideas, and finding transitional phrases to hold her ideas together. She did none of this in isolation. Over a two-and-a-half-week period she worked in cooperation with many others: Luanne, Robert Frost, Zandy and Theresa, me. Having accomplished this essay in cooperation today, the chances are pretty good that Laura can do it alone tomorrow—if someone in grade nine will give her a chance.

In eighth grade Laura completed twenty-one pieces of writing encompassing many genres. She read thirty-one novels. Her classmates and I expected her to do these things and gave her all the time and help she needed to achieve, and she did. The *environment* marched ahead of Laura and led her. It is an environment that cannot be replicated in a resource room or in a tracked class of slow learners. Laura was surrounded by people writing and conferring and publishing, by high expectations, by good children's literature, by energy, commitment, and a willingness on the part of her teacher to be patient and give the time and response that special writers need.

For the sake of the Lauras in our schools, students working alone with limited opportunities to show what they can do, it is time that we pierce the mystique surrounding special education students and invite them, and their teachers, to join us—to acknowledge and embrace the rich, varied, and purposeful processes of writing and reading and the rich, varied, and purposeful ways that our students will learn writing and reading. In cooperation, we all have something to learn.

3 ▶ READING, WRITING, AND THINKING

ONE MORNING IN JUNE, IN THE MIDST OF THE HURLY-BURLY OF a junior high homeroom, I glanced up from the mess of forms and memos that land on a homeroom teacher's desk to see Kelli standing silently before me. Kelli is one of those kids who usually smiles, but today her face was a stone. Before I could speak, she reached into her pocket, pulled out a wad of folded paper, and held it out to me. She whispered, "Would you read this? It's about *him.*" I looked at her face a second longer, then unfolded and smoothed the page. When I looked up again, she was gone. But I knew now who *he* was and why Kelli wasn't smiling today.

The evening news programs had been filled with the bad news. A children's poet—whose books my students treasured, whose tricks they borrowed for poems of their own, whose annual readings at our school brought down the house—had been indicted on charges of child abuse. Of all my eighth graders, Kelli had been the most fanatical in her admiration. She had learned from him how to read poetry and how to write it. Now, worse than ever before, she was betrayed by an adult. Kelli's note to me was a poem, her response to yesterday's bad news.

FOOTSTEPS TO FOLLOW

What happened to all the Lone Rangers,
The heroes on their white stallions,
The knights in white armor who
Fought for our honor?

Where have all the good guys gone?
Whose footsteps are we to follow in now?
Whose shoes are we to fill?
Mine is the voice of this generation—
The voice of a thousand.
Do you hear our unanswered questions?
Are you so deaf that you cannot hear?
So what happened to you, Lone Ranger?
Each time you don't answer, a little
Part of us dies.

There is no neat or easy resolution here. Kelli knew that her question would not be answered because she knows there is no answer. Asking the question is enough. Finding language that gives shape to her anger and uncertainty—imagining the metaphor that serves as a prism for her to explore her feelings—is more than enough. Kelli used writing to discover what she thinks about a subject that matters. For her, thinking and writing are inseparable. Both are essential to how she lives her life.

I can't resist contrasting Kelli's thoughtfulness with the brand of thinking I see more and more emphasized in in-service courses and commercial programs. Completely in spite of myself I find I have become an expert in something called "critical thinking skills." Two journals devoted to critical thinking skills bombard our post office box with subscription offers, and at least once a month my junk mail includes a brochure that advertises the latest in materials that will "teach every student the critical thinking skills so essential to competing in today's fast-paced world." For just pennies a day I can buy "ready-to-use lesson plans and state-of-the-art teaching strategies" in micro and macro thinking, divergent thinking, affective awareness, hypothesis formulation, verbal sequences and verbal classifications, syllogisms, heuristics, and something called logical reasoning fallacies. Or I can address the ever-popular eight learning styles, not to be confused with the six learning styles, the four learning styles, or, from the world of neuropsychology, the hemispheric preference model. My students will deduct and induct or my money back. Then they will "learn to apply their new skills to a variety of classroom situations in every subject area." And, by a lucky coincidence, the same publishers will sell me a test that measures critical thinking abilities. They even offer programs of "cognitive therapy" for the unfortunate students in my classroom who flunk thinking.

Publishers are quick to spot trends. It's their business. They know that the National Assessment of Educational Progress keeps turning up students who can't or won't go beyond surface features to analyze and evaluate what they read, students who can't or won't go beyond the givens of a writing assignment to explore and organize complexities—in short, students who do not make cognitive leaps. So what better way to inspire cognitive leaps than to institute a new mastery program of thinking skills in your school or district? (We can schedule it from 9:00 to 9:30, between the mandated "Say No to Drugs" lesson and the mandated "Study Skills for Today" unit.)

Commercial programs have one essential message: divide and conquer. In the face of decades of research that shows that students learn best in whole, meaningful situations, programs give us scope and sequence. They provide grade-by-grade rules and forms, and we cover their curricula, one so-called skill at a time. And it does not work. Yet superintendents, principals, curriculum coordinators, department heads—and classroom teachers, too—continue to buy commercial programs that turn teachers and students into puppets.

Many teachers are trying to break this cycle. What we need is ammunition so that we can come back at the faceless committees that write language arts programs, the marketing experts who call themselves educational researchers, and the misinformed powers-that-be who assign the programs, to come back armed with two kinds of knowledge that Frank Smith (1978) defines as essential to our cause.

First, we need to know about language processes, about the wonderfully diverse, complicated, and idiosyncratic things that writers and readers actually do when they use language to make meaning. These processes bear little relation to the activities prescribed in textbooks. Mary Ellen Giacobbe's analysis of language arts texts (1988) shows publishers misapplying all the new terminology of writing process in an attempt to dress up the same tired old collection of context-stripped exercises.

Second, we need to know the individual writers and readers in our classrooms. We need to know how to observe their experiences as learners and make sense of what we see in ways that will move a learner forward. We cannot know these things if our only perspective on students is through a tunnel of textbooks, workbooks, worksheets, and software.

The new programs of thinking skills only add insult to this injury. While the language arts programs rob us of our expertise as readers and writers, the critical thinking materials rob us of our powers as critical thinkers. The materials spell out exactly what and how we should teach and students should learn. In short, they tell us not to think in order to teach our students how to think. Even worse, because the program content consists of artificial and sterile exercises, students are mostly asked to think about nothing.

People think about something. They think hardest and best when it is something that matters to them. In school, kids think in breathtaking ways when they have an investment—when there's something at stake—in what they are being asked to do and when what they are being asked to do makes sense. They do not acquire and transfer thinking skills to appropriate situations any more than they acquire and transfer bits of grammatical trivia to their genuine writing and speaking occasions.

People learn in meaningful contexts. In the English classroom, students become *thoughtful* readers, writers, and speakers when they engage in tasks that are useful, interesting, complex, and significant. That is a tall order, one we are beginning to be able to fill thanks to the work of an ever-expanding group of teachers, researchers, and theorists—Glenda Bissex, Toby Fulwiler, Mary Ellen Giacobbe, Dixie Goswami, Donald Graves, Jane Hansen, Jerry Harste, Don Holdaway, Donald Murray, Thomas Newkirk, Frank Smith—none of whom has a program to sell us. In the face of data that show teachers outtalk kids by a ratio of three to one (Goodlad 1984), this new body of work focuses on what happens when teachers turn over class time to students' writing, reading, and talk. In the face of data that show that instruction that invites open response—in other words, critical thinking—makes up less than 1 percent of our teaching (Goodlad 1984), their work describes student-teacher conferences in which students think aloud about their intentions, plans, and processes. In this other kind of classroom, students of all ages, kindergarten through college, can make astonishing cognitive leaps. Here, Donald Murray (1982) says, students have "the terrible freedom" to think and to act. Teachers have a terrible freedom, too: to stop teaching programs and start responding to what our kids are actually thinking and doing.

No program could have elicited Kelli's poem "Footsteps to Follow." The occasion, form, voice, tensions, and metaphors are Kelli's own. As an English teacher, it took me a very long time to learn this. Neither can the environment in which Kelli wrote "Footsteps to Follow" be purchased through a catalogue. It took me an even longer time to discover and organize the elements that would re-create my classroom as a place where students could use language to think. This special place is a reading and writing workshop, and its central elements are time, choice, and response (Giacobbe 1986).

Kelli and her classmates had time every day to read and write in school. Their reading and writing replaced listening to me talk about reading and writing as the most important activities in the classroom. We know that fluent readers and effective writers are people who have practiced these skills in genuine situations. When we make time for these activities, we create the possibility that all of our students will read with understanding and appreciation and write with clarity and grace.

Kelli and her classmates made choices. They developed their own subjects for writing, their own purposes and audiences, and set their own pace. They selected their own books and read at their own pace. They made a personal investment every day in what they were writing and reading, and because they cared, they worked and thought hard.

Finally, Kelli and her classmates had opportunities for response before and while they read and wrote, not merely at the end, when it was too late for my advice to do them much good. I responded to them and they to each other in conferences: brief, frequent dialogues with writers and readers about what they have done and what they might do next.

Over the course of the school year these eighth graders finished an average of twenty pieces of writing representing many genres: poetry, editorials, short fiction, reviews, correspondence of all kinds, parodies, novels, computer programs, scripts, children's books, feature articles, time capsule lists, contest entries, original research, petitions, intercom announcements, résumés, interviews, and eulogies. They read an average of thirty-five books representing many authors: C. S. Lewis, J. D. Salinger, e e cummings, L. M. Montgomery, and S. E. Hinton; Robert Frost, Louis L'Amour, Robert Lipsyte, Susan Beth Pfeffer, Cynthia Voigt, Anne Tyler, Ursula K. LeGuin, Farley Mowat, and Jack London.

Students' thinking was at the heart of all of it. Any act of *genuine* authorship or *genuine* reading or *genuine* conversation is interwoven with and inseparable from *genuine* thought. In James Britton's phrase, language is nothing less than "the exposed edge of thought." Recently I returned to my students' work to try to uncover how they think critically as readers and writers, to look at what shows up when kids are expected, and helped, to think for themselves in their English classes.

Mike is a rabid sports fan. He is also a typical adolescent, tempted by every mail-order ad he reads. If the ad promises something to do with professional baseball, basketball, or football, he succumbs. One fall, he got stung. He watched his mail every day for the commemorative envelopes he had paid for and was supposed to receive. Every day they didn't arrive. And then he got a bill for an additional payment. Mike came to school angry. He brought with him a copy of the original offer and the company's latest bill, and for three class periods he read and reread the fine print in the ad and worked on drafts of a letter to the company, trying to describe exactly what had happened and what he wanted them to do. He pulled a folder from the classroom resource library that showed how to set up a formal business letter. This is the letter he finally sent.

———— Avenue
Boothbay, Maine 04537
October 8

National Baseball Foundation
P. O. Box 3
Amawalk, New York 10501

Dear Sirs:

This letter concerns the commemorative envelopes offer I subscribed to.

I am confused. The offer states that for $15.95 I receive at least seven commemorative envelopes and a free album.

On May 14, I sent a check (check number 2063) for $15.95 for the seven envelopes. Now I have received a bill for an additional $15.95, and I have only received the album and one of the envelopes (Nolan Ryan).

As I have already paid the $15.95, I expect to receive the remainder of the envelopes as promised. If that is not possible, I will return the envelope of Nolan Ryan and I would like my money to be refunded.

I await your earliest possible response. Thank you.

Sincerely yours,
Michael

The National Baseball Foundation sent six additional envelopes at the end of the month.

For a boy who claims to be confused, Mike has done an effective job of analyzing, characterizing, and solving a problem. He marshals the facts of his case, presents his evidence, and tells what he expects will happen. I might be tempted to see this as just another little business letter, but because I am currently in the midst of my own war of correspondence with Sears, Roebuck over a carpet I have yet to receive and for which they keep billing me, I know how hard it is to unscramble a situation, set it out for others' comprehension, and do it with brevity and clarity. As a writer, Mike did the hard work of casting and recasting his thoughts because he had something at stake—his pride, but also $15.95.

Tiffany, one of Mike's classmates, was a remedial reader mainstreamed into the English program. Because students are choosing their own topics and books, because teaching and learning are truly individualized, special education and remedial students can enter the workshop and pursue their own interests at their own pace, and they can succeed. Tiffany also wrote a business letter; hers was addressed to Simon & Schuster. She was upset that their edition of Anne Frank's *Diary* included an insert, bound into the middle of the book, that gave background information on Anne's life and times—and her death. This first-time reader of the *Diary* discovered much sooner than she expected to what happened to the inhabitants of the Secret Annex.

Box ———
Boothbay Harbor, Maine 04538
April 14

Simon & Schuster, Inc.
1230 Avenue of the Americas
New York, New York 10020

Dear Sir:

I finished reading your book *Anne Frank: The Diary of a Young Girl* a while back.

The background on Anne Frank was put in the middle of the book. It cut a sentence from her diary in half and broke my train of thought. I think it was put in the wrong spot. Also, some of the things about her background told you what was going to happen later in the book. I think if it was necessary to insert the part about her background, it should have been put at the end.

Besides that, I thought it was a very good book because Anne was so honest and wasn't afraid to tell the truth about how she felt.

I've heard that *Anne Frank: The Diary of a Young Girl* wasn't her complete diary, that her father took things out he felt were inappropriate, and that her whole diary was going to be released soon. I would be very interested to hear when it is to be released, if it is so.

Thank you for your time.

Sincerely yours,
Tiffany

The publishers of reading programs do not receive many letters like Tiffany's. Students who read textbook prose seldom react as Tiffany reacts. She is a passionate reader, one who makes choices and acts on them. Because she makes choices as a writer and reader, she is aware that professional authors and editors are not infallible—they are people like her who make choices too, and sometimes she thinks their choices are wrong. But Tiffany does more than react to the format of this edition of the *Diary*. She evaluates the book, and she tries to track down a rumor about the release of an unabridged edition.

Over the years Tiffany received much remediation designed to help her "decode" printed texts, none of which engaged her as *Anne Frank* did. When Tiffany reads this whole, rich piece of literature that she selected, she does much more than decode. She criticizes, evaluates, speculates, and participates in the larger literary community.

Although students' ideas for writing result in many different genres, narrative is a consistently popular form. They write what they enjoy reading—stories—and sometimes their narratives describe their own experiences. Students who write begin to see their lives as stories, as material to be contemplated and shaped. But they do more than tell stories. They think about the significances of their experiences and use writing as a way to reflect on and characterize the events of their lives, as Heather does in "True or False."

TRUE OR FALSE

"Hmmmm . . . -9 is greater than $-3 + \frac{1}{3}$. True or false? Well, first you would . . ." my concentration on my math was interrupted by a loud screech and three loud howls from outside. I looked out my window and saw a dog in the middle of the opposite side of the road.

"Mom, Mom!" I said as I ran down the stairs.

"I'm in the bathroom giving Jessica a bath."

As I opened the door I said, "Mom, a dog just got hit by a car, and . . . "

"Run down and tell your father," she said before I could even finish my sentence.

I ran downstairs, practically falling down them. "Dad, Dad!"

"Shhh! I'm on the phone!"

"But, Dad! A dog just got hit by a car and it's hurt!"

He looked under the table to make sure it wasn't our dog. "Are there people out there with it?"

"Yeah."

"Well, I'm on the phone! Let the people who are out there take care of it. They probably already called the vet's. Now get upstairs and finish your homework!"

As I stumbled up the stairs, I thought about the poor dog outside. Did he have an owner? I didn't think so. I'd seen him on the street but I'd never seen him with anyone. I got to the third floor and sat at my desk. It was right in front of the window. I sat there and watched. A blue truck pulled up and a guy hopped out. The dog was now wrapped in a blanket. The guy picked up the dog, dumped him in the back of the truck, and took off. I saw a little puddle of blood from where the dog had been lying. I pulled the shade down and went back to my math.

"-9 is greater than $-3 + \frac{1}{3}$. True or false?"

That would be false.

Heather's conclusion contains no earnest moralizing; it is abrupt on purpose. She wants us to think when we finish reading her story, to pause for a moment and consider the implications of her experience—the callousness she found around her and then in herself, too. In this piece Heather began to discover that between true and false and black and white there are cloudy areas—questions of responsibility that do not have easy answers. And she draws on her reading in developing her theme. The good fiction and poetry that she is reading every day are teaching her subtlety, a technique no one ever learned from a program or a worksheet.

Some of the thinking that shows up in students' writing is less than subtle, as adolescents' humor tends to be less than subtle. A popular kind of writing among eighth graders, for whom caricature is a way of life, is parody, where they borrow the form of someone else's writing but twist it for their own purposes. If it is to work, parody requires a writer to know another's writing inside out, to read analytically and then to synthesize the original work in an original work of his or her own. Mike analyzed and synthesized Bryan Adams's song "Heaven" to write a version he titled "Kevin." Kevin is Mike's classmate and a local hero; he was practically the only eighth grader to score any points all season long for Boothbay's junior high football team. Line for line and syllable for syllable, Mike used the lyrics of "Heaven" to celebrate "Kevin." The chorus is particularly stirring:

CHORUS

Kevin, you're all that we want
When you're running for touchdowns.
And we're finding it hard to believe
That you're a mortal, not sent from heaven.
And touchdowns are all that we need,
And we found them there in your feet.
It isn't too hard to believe . . .
The best is Kevin.

One Tuesday morning before school started Mike organized a meeting of all the boys on the football team, minus Kevin. They met with a tape recorder. Mike passed out copies of his lyrics and recorded the team singing his ode to Kev, which they played over the loudspeaker at practice that night. Kevin about died.

I remember the underground writing that I did in high school with my friends: the parodies of letters from the assistant principal that I wrote, typed, and mailed to my friends' parents and the by-laws of "The Bluebirds," the ludicrous mock sorority that we organized to counter the ludicrous real sororities at my school. This summer my mother cleaned out the closet in my old bedroom and found a series of FBI reports on my movements as a high school sophomore, written by Janet Murphy, my best friend and a genuine wit. Although we shared this writing in school, covertly, we wrote it outside of school. In school, we answered essay questions.

Part of the richness of our students' lives is their play, including language play. If we make room for it in our classrooms, we can help students use writing to recognize, think about, and comment on the ridiculous in their worlds. We can help them be clever. Programmed instructional approaches do not inspire wit or bring the underground curriculum aboveground.

As Mike synthesized another author's form to play with it, students were constantly borrowing from their reading in their writing. Because they read so widely and because I had learned to make available as great a range of literature as I could provide them, read aloud to them, and talked about the ways that writers crafted their works, students began to draw on other authors' themes, techniques, and language. I learned from their borrowings why reading and writing belong together. Time and again they demonstrated the phenomenon that Frank Smith (1988) calls "reading like a writer." I learned they did not need me to sponsor structured exercises or assign models. Given opportunities to discover and act on their own intentions as readers and writers, students naturally made connections.

In their reading workshop, students also wrote specifically in response to what they were reading. They and I exchanged letters, thousands of letters back and forth about books, authors, reading, and writing. These replaced book reports—the dullest writing I have ever read—and allowed students and me to meet and talk on common ground. More importantly, because the talk was written down, students were able to go deeper, to become less plot-bound and more critical than in oral conversation. Chatting on paper helped them to reflect, to think about their thinking. Answering their letters helped me to reflect, too. In this exchange with Justine I developed a theory about the novels of V. C. Andrews. I am not sure that I want to have a theory about V. C. Andrews, but my writing helped me understand why her writing can exert such power over readers.

Ms. A.,

I finished *My Sweet Audrina* by V.C. Andrews. Sandy told me she read an article saying Andrews was vulgar. I didn't agree then, but I do now.

She's a good plotter, terrible writer (like you say Stephen King is). It was just one unbelievable happening after another. It held you there, but I wouldn't recommend it.

Justine

Dear Justine,

You're so smart. And you're so right. Why don't you take over this class and I'll retire to Bermuda?

I think V. C. Andrews is the most vulgar of the vulgar. I also know teachers (yes, here at BRES) who are hooked on her books. Readers seem to be so intrigued by the depth of her vulgarity that they read on to see exactly how much more disgusting she can get. I read one of her novels, and my best analogy for the experience is quicksand. I was laughing and groaning at her style but unable to resist finding out how the book ended. Afterward I felt sick, as if I'd eaten two chocolate cakes whole.

There's a side of people—of myself—I'll never understand: the side that will watch a building on fire and read V. C. Andrews.

Ms. A.

All of this is first-draft writing, unpolished and unrevised. It has the informality and spontaneity of notes passed in class, with a special difference. Students and I use the letters as an occasion to theorize about literature, to wonder what works of literature mean to our lives, and why. Figure 3–1 shows my Christmas card from Alice—or, rather, it was supposed to be a Christmas card. Because Alice has come to regard our correspondence as a vehicle

---

FIGURE 3–1

Alice's Christmas Greeting

'☺' MERRY CHRISTMAS!   12/20

Dear Ms. Atwell,

You said we could write, so I figured right now was the the perfect time. You see, I just finished I am the Cheese, it's 2:00 a.m, and I refuse to go to bed. That book scares me a lot, it's so different, so sad. I tried to explain my feelings to my Mom but she hasn't ever read the book. She says it's a book about paranoia etc. It was so scary, I find myself wondering – could this really happen? Is it a joke? The ending, it came so quickly, the explanation for the bike ride. I still haven't figured out if Amy Herty was a fragment of his imagination. What a scary book.

Holiday Greetings

Well, Merry Christmas, Happy New Year, etc.

Your Student,
Alice '☺'

for thinking, she can't stop. She has learned to figure things out in her writing; in the card she is trying to make her own meaning of *I Am the Cheese.*

Again, the problem with programmed instruction is that it limits what kids can do. It cheats them. Scope and sequence can never include everything of which our students are capable. And it can never allow for the obsessions that are so much a part of learning, when something hooks us and we become deeply involved and pursue it singlemindedly, as Alice did.

Students who are asked to read, write, and think about reading and writing go *inside* books where they actively engage, analyzing and evaluating rather than summarizing plot. Donald Murray has said that in a writing workshop we are really teaching our students to be readers. Writers in the workshop are probably the most critical of all readers, both of their own and others' emerging texts. The reverse also holds true. In reading workshop, I am teaching students to be writers. I hope that they will go beyond plot, stop letting stories happen to them, and start making decisions about what is and isn't working in pieces of their reading, this other kind of emerging text.

We are learning that across the disciplines, creative thinkers are less problem solvers than problem *finders.* I think that this should be our universal goal as teachers of English: to help our students, as writers and readers, find the problems that matter to them; to stop postponing the complex, interesting stuff in the name of "giving kids the basics" or "providing a foundation" and acknowledge that we learn the basics in pursuit of the interesting stuff.

What steps can we take? First, we need to reject impoverished models that promise skills mastery, to *just say no* to programs, worksheets, workbooks, and exercises, to say no more dummy runs when we can be giving kids the real thing. We need to learn about writing and reading processes by reading the best in our field but also by reading *and writing* literature for ourselves, for our own pleasures and purposes, our own letters, stories, poetry, opinions. When we know these processes from the inside, we can extend generous, sensible invitations to our students to join us in a literate community. And we can observe our students. What do they do as writers and readers? What do they know? What do they need to know next? What do they *love*?

Love isn't a word used much these days in connection with curriculum, either among textbook publishers or, sadly, us process types. It is the word Seymour Papert (1980) chose in the foreword to *Mindstorms*, his book about children, computers, thinking, and learning. Papert recounts how as a toddler he became obsessed with gears, playing with gear sets and figuring out how they worked. In school he used gears as his own private models for more abstract ideas, like the multiplication tables and equations with two variables. One day he was surprised to discover that most adults didn't understand, or even care about, the magic of the gears. And he began to formulate a fundamental fact about learning: "Anything is easy if you can assimilate it to your collection of models. If you can't, anything can be painfully difficult. . . . What an individual can learn, and how he learns it, depends on what model he has available" (vii). Papert concludes:

> A modern-day Montessori might propose, if convinced by my story, to create a gear set for children. Thus every child might have the experience I had. But to hope for this would be to miss the essence of the story. *I fell in love with the gears.* This is something that cannot be reduced to purely "cognitive" terms. Something very personal happened, and one cannot assume that it would be repeated for other children in exactly the same form. (viii)

As teachers of writing, reading, and thinking, perhaps we are posing the wrong questions. Instead of asking, "Which program is the best? Whose scope and sequence will produce the highest scores?" we might wonder, "What models of reading and writing are available to my students? Are they varied and genuine and fascinating?" Or better yet, "How can my teaching be flexible enough so that every child can create his or her own version of the gears?" Or, best of all, "How do I teach so that each of my students can fall in love with language?"

4 WHEN READERS RESPOND

U NDER THE INFLUENCE OF THOMAS NEWKIRK (1989) AND HIS daughter Sarah, I began recording stories about my daughter's literacy when Anne was sixteen months old. It was around that time that I began to appreciate the influence of literature on what she says and does and the range of her transactions with literature—some in spite of other readers (usually me and her father), some because of other readers, and some that have to do only with Anne herself.

A favorite author of all three of us is Shirley Hughes, who has written four books about a young sister and brother named Lucy and Tom. *Lucy and Tom's 1.2.3.* (1987) is a gentle math concept book in which mathematical principles are embedded in a particularly subtle and engaging way. One Sunday afternoon I was making lasagna and Anne was perched on the kitchen counter, determined to help me with dinner. Then, in response to an illustration from the Hughes book that shows Lucy and Tom racing toy cars of different sizes down a ramp, she asked for one of the uncooked noodles, clambered down off the counter, and clambered back up again with four Matchbox cars. She used the noodle to make a ramp between a mixing bowl and spice box, predicted which little car would travel the farthest, then shot the cars down the noodle. Imagine her parents' smug faces as we watched Anne apply the lessons of the book to her real life.

However, Anne doesn't always wish to apply the lessons that we take from her books. Her babysitter was pregnant, and for months Anne and her three-year-old friends had been shoving dolls under their shirts and whining about their varicose veins—which they interpreted, not inaccurately, as "very close." So I bought her Millicent Selsam's *From Egg to Chick* (1946), a book about a birth cycle. Anne liked the book all right, but she positively lit up when the newborn chick's feathers had dried and turned fluffy. Then she reached out two fingers and stroked the photograph like mad. I wanted her to learn about birth; she wanted to pat the chickie.

However, she does learn from her books. *The Stopwatch* is a book by David Lloyd (1986) that explores sibling rivalry. Anne used it to attempt to teach herself how to stand on her head. She studied the cover and endpapers, which show a brother and sister performing headstands, tried a few herself, returned to the book, and studied the illustrations some more. She actually learned how to do a forward roll from the pictures in Marc Brown's *D. W. Flips* (1987). Anne also has a special library that was initiated by a gift from Donald Murray before she was born, an assortment of blank books in which she writes and from which she likes to read. One morning she opened a blank book and announced, "I'm reading about salad—so I can like it better." A few days later she tore a piece of lettuce off my shrimp cocktail and nibbled at it. I asked, "What do you think?" She spit it out and said, "I think I'm going to have to do some more reading!" She knows the power of the printed word to open minds and to teach.

However, the power of books is not only in the knowledge that readers derive. Anne's books are also powerful social tools, a way of creating instant community. Choosing the books to pack for her babysitter to read aloud was a major decision as she weighed her friends' interests and tried to anticipate their tastes. She reported that Rachel Isadora's ballet books had been a *perfect* choice after she and her equally ballerina-obsessed friends had practiced the five positions together during that day's read-aloud. Her books are another way for her to relate to her friends, and to us. Anne liked Mairi Hedderwick's books about Katie Morag, but she knew that her father loved them. Whenever she wanted to appease Toby or create a special time for them alone, she offered, "Would you like to read me a Katie Morag story?" He always said yes.

However, no matter how much I complained about the story of Cinderella, no matter how clear I made my disdain for this

cheerful, passive wimp of a character, Anne asked for her Cinderella books again and again. She opened her eyes and mouth in
exaggerated shock every time the stepsisters taunted "Cinder-
britches," she smirked every time they came home from the ball
to report about the beautiful stranger, and she shivered with
pleasure every time she recited, in chorus with me, "And it fit,
perfectly."

Anne is not going through a cute phase as a reader. She
doesn't lack discipline or taste, and she will never come to her
senses and read like me or Toby or anybody. She reads in all of
the ways that Anne reads and as a member of the various communities of which Anne is a member. At any age or stage, what is
important about a work of literature is an individual matter—
including whether a work is important at all.

As more teachers abandon basals and anthologies and turn
to trade books, we are seeing more readers like Anne: for example, students who don't connect with the literature that we want
them to read. I have talked with teachers who were disap-
pointed—upset, even—with those of their kids who hadn't liked
The Indian in the Cupboard (Banks 1980) or *To Kill a Mockingbird*
(Lee 1960). Or we see students who connect with literature that
we don't want them to read: witness the hullaballoo from teachers and parents about the popularity of Ann Martin's Babysitters
Club series or Stephen King. Or we see kids who don't "get" a
book the way we think they should, who don't understand the
mystery of the Jack Frost figure in Chris Van Allsburg's *The
Stranger* (1986) but seem to like the book anyway. (Anne didn't
know who Jack Frost was or care much, for that matter. When we
read *The Stranger*, it was so she could become Katy Bailey.) Or we
see kids whose responses are so different from our own that they
surely must be recalcitrant or insolent or even not very bright,
because no matter what we say about the humane and wonderful
qualities with which E. B. White endows Charlotte and Wilbur,
to these readers it's still "that stupid book about a boring spider
and a gross pig."

The point is that none of these readers is wrong. Again,
what is *important* about a work of literature is an individual matter. Making the shift from textbooks to literature requires more
than trading one set of books for another. I think that Louise
Rosenblatt's work in the area of reader response can be of particular help in showing how the kinds of responses to reading that

we encourage—or discourage—and the ways that we meet the child's response are the factors that will make or break a literature-based reading program.

Rosenblatt's literary theory first appeared over fifty years ago in her book *Literature as Exploration* (1938). She described reading as a *transaction* between a reader and a text in which reader and text make an equal contribution. Rosenblatt observes that reading is a "synthesis of what the reader already knows and feels and desires with what the literary text offers" (272). The literary work of art is never merely the graphic symbols on the page. Rather the "poem," as she calls a work of literature, exists only in the "live circuit" between a reader and a text.

Emerson wrote, "One must be an inventor to read well. . . . There is then creative reading as well as creative writing." In Rosenblatt's theory, the creative reader infuses meaning into the symbols, but the text channels that meaning through the way that it is constructed. To be sure, it is the text that stimulates and regulates the reader's response, but that response is organized around the reader's experiences, the reader's abilities, and the reader's tastes—as Anne's responses to her books are based on the way that Anne's mind meets these texts.

In a speech that is included in her book *The Spying Heart* (1989), the novelist Katherine Paterson describes the live circuit between a reader and a text:

> A seventh-grader in California asked me, "What do you want the reader to achieve by reading *Bridge to Terabithia?*" And I said to him, "Look, my job is to write the best book I know how to write. Your job is to decide what you're to achieve by reading it." A book is a cooperative venture. The writer can write a story down, but the book will never be complete until a reader of whatever age takes that book and brings it to his own story. I realize tonight, as I realize every time I speak, that I am addressing an audience that includes many of my coauthors.
>
> So please don't ask me where I get my ideas as if I were some creature foreign to you who drinks at an alien watering trough. Don't ask me where I get my ideas as though you have no part, no responsibility, in bringing what you read to life. . . . It is only when the deepest

sound going forth from my heart meets the deepest sound coming forth from yours—it is only in this encounter that the true music begins. (36–37)

When we listen to Paterson speak of the true music of reading literature, "decoding" becomes worse than a misnomer. Decoding denies the reader a role. It reduces reading to a mechanical translation of letters to sounds and implies that there is a single, unambiguous relationship between words on the page and meaning. Decoding reveals that the individual reader is merely a conduit programmed to have X response, understand X symbols, carry away X information, and find X significance.

I have a personal photocopier in my office. It runs on cartridges that must be changed every two thousand copies. The instructions for this operation are written, I assume, to be as literal and unambiguous as possible. But in four years I have successfully changed a cartridge just once: this last time around. Step 4 of the instructions reads, "Hold the new cartridge firmly, fold the tab down, and peel off the vinyl sealing tape completely by pulling out on the tab." I was unable to make these words fit my copier. I couldn't envision folding down and pulling out as part of the same operation. I broke off the whole tab every time, which snapped the sealing tape, which led to three-quarters of an hour with a pair of needle-nosed pliers trying to remove this strip of plastic from inside the cartridge. Toby finally read the instructions, envisioned the procedure, and, like a good teacher, showed me how to fold down and pull out on the tab at the same time. If reading were mere decoding, I would have understood what Toby understood—what, apparently, everyone else who owns one of these machines understood. For better or for worse, reading isn't nearly so straightforward.

Readers really run into trouble when we come to writing that is purposely ambiguous—when we try to pretend that a short story has *a* main idea, that a fairy tale or fable has *a* moral, or that a poem has *a* significance.

As part of a course I taught on response to reading, forty high school and university English teachers and I mapped our way through our reading of a poem that none of us had read before. This was an activity described in "Looking for Trouble," an article by Tom Newkirk (1990) about the myth of the inspired reader, the mystique that denies the real, messy process of reading a poem. We all fumble at first readings; we all experience uncertainty, confusion, and difficulty. But our students seldom know this. Instead, they get our polished performances and full-blown analyses, and they believe themselves deficient as readers of poetry because they're unable to achieve instant understanding.

My husband found a poem, removed the poet's name, made forty-one copies, and distributed them to my class and me. Following Newkirk's procedures we individually read and reread the poem and marked the lines that gave us difficulty with each consecutive reading; the first time through I marked more than half of the poem. Then we each wrote a narrative account of the reading, using the markings to cue our memories about the first reading, the second, the third, and so on. This is called a protocol.

The poem was Randall Jarrell's "The Woman at the Washington Zoo" (1968). When some of us read aloud our protocols, no two were even remotely similar accounts of the process of reading the poem. Our interpretations of what the poem was about were almost as different. We couldn't even agree about the identity of the speaker. We were expert readers who spent regular time, thirty-five weeks a year, discussing literature, and our responses to the poem were as personal and idiosyncratic as Anne's to her books. But then, through listening to each other's responses, returning to the text, and coming back to talk about it over the next few days, we did agree about the "meaning" of the text—who the speaker is, why she speaks as she does, what it is she wants. But we never agreed about the *significance* of the poem—or about whether we liked it. I'll come back to this point.

Rosenblatt differentiates the two kinds of reading I've described in my anecdotes about the photocopier instructions and the Jarrell poem as *efferent* and *aesthetic*. When we engage in efferent reading, we are seeking to carry away information from the text: what to do in installing a new photocopier cartridge. When we read aesthetically, our attention is on what is being "lived through" during the reading: on our reaction to the anguish of the woman at the zoo and to the threat and attraction of the natural world that the animals represent. In efferent reading we are more likely to ask *who* does *what, where, when, why,* and *to what effect.* In aesthetic reading we wonder, "How did you feel and think? And *why* did you feel and think it? What in the text are you responding to?"

The importance of Rosenblatt's work for us, as teachers making a shift away from basals, anthologies, workbooks, and teacher's manual questions, is in making sure that we don't basalize the literature to which we now turn in their stead. By that I mean asking basal questions of the literature our students are reading.

By and large, workbooks and teacher's manuals call for efferent reading by asking the student to carry away information from the literary text. Even in the new basal readers that include excerpts from literature—much of it "basalized," as Ken Goodman (1987) has shown us—the response that is called for is still text-centered, is *still efferent:* Who is the main character? When did she get new clothes? What happened at the end? Which character is bigger? As Lee Galda (1988) has pointed out, these questions are really designed to tell us whether or not students have read the selection.

The individual teacher who is trying to abandon commercial programs must also abandon an insidious, long-standing way of perceiving and responding to literature. He or she must trade a style of instruction that calls for efferent reading for opportunities for aesthetic modes of response. This is easier said than done.

A teacher that I know well began to teach writing process in her twentieth year of teaching. She embraced writing workshop methods wholeheartedly and effectively; she worked on pieces of her own writing, read about the teaching of writing, and spoke and published about her classroom. What a leap this was for her—to go from nothing, from almost no writing, to such an incredible something.

Two years ago, my friend braced herself for another leap. She decided to do away with basal readers and run a literature-based reading program. So she shelved the anthologies, bought a wonderful classroom library, and waited for the magic. It never came.

My friend had been asking efferent questions of readers for twenty-seven years. She had defined reading and reading comprehension according to commercial programs for twenty-seven years. The prejudices she had to overcome were deeper and more pervasive than any she had ever encountered in changing her view of writing or her ways of teaching writing. And she is having a hard time. She wonders: How can she make sure that her students are getting what they're supposed to be getting from

these books? That they're recalling details? Understanding cause
and effect? Learning new vocabulary? Drawing appropriate infer-
ences? *Really* reading the books?

Only if she asks them. And so her literature program
revolves around students' written responses (in dialogue journals)
and oral responses (in conferences) to the familiar mode of *who*
did *what, when, where, why,* and *to what effect.*

Ken Goodman tells the story of asking a Navajo boy why he
thought Scott O'Dell had written *Sing Down the Moon* (1977), a
novel of the Navajo people that he'd just read. The boy
responded, "To teach me new words." Ken also describes a group
of sixth graders who complained about the questions that followed a basal revision of a Jack London story. The teacher asked
the kids who they thought had written the questions, and the
kids responded, "Jack London." Well, then why weren't there
questions at the end of London's short stories that weren't in
basals? Simple. Because in this story he was teaching them to
read. "Besides," one boy said, "he wants to be sure you're paying
attention." In Figure 4–1, a second-grade writer has already
learned from her basal reading program how to make sure that her
own readers are paying attention.

Children learn what we teach them. If the literature-based
reading program is really a skills-based reading program, they will
learn that literature is to be used to learn so-called reading skills,
not to make music. The students in my friend's classroom try to
avoid reading conferences with their teacher. Their dialogue
journal entries are perfunctory answers to questions about plot,
cause and effect, and main ideas. And the affect is flat. There are
few live circuits between children and texts in this room. Their
teacher sees this but does not know what to do with a book except
ask questions that sound as if they came straight from a teacher's
manual.

Ken Goodman has noted that the question paradigm in
teacher's manuals "appears to be based on a view that children
comprehend to the extent that they agree with the question
writer's view of the text meaning." He says, further, that "even
when the question is intended to draw on 'background knowledge' or require 'critical thinking,' a simple, conformist answer is
suggested as a model for the teacher of what answers to accept"
(1987, 35). So an aesthetic response is precluded because even
the "higher level" questions are based on someone else's experi-

FIGURE 4-1

A Second-Grade Writer Learns from Her Reading Program

The Apples

I had an apple tree.
Every spring I go and pick
some apples. But one spring
the apples didn't grow
it was very dispointy!
Finely, I asked my mom
why the apples didnot grow?
She said, "Because the tree
died!" I said, "What!"
Well winter came our tree was
died. We had no apples to
eat. Then spring came again.
We planted a new apple tree. It
was beautiful. Now we had
about 10 dozen of apples. They
were dillishis.

The end!

Turn over.

What died? _____
Did she have a mom? _____
What did they have nothing of ___
What did she do every spring?
_____

ence of reading the text. As Rosenblatt has written, someone else can summarize a report for us, but "no one can read a poem for us" (1938, 33).

I think that it's in this regard that Rosenblatt's work may be of most value to teachers of reading. We can examine the kinds of questions we ask before and after students read literature. Do our questions bypass readers' attention to what they feel and think about a text? Do we ask students to carry away information from the literary text, or to find and agree with someone else's meaning? And we can reexamine our definition of comprehension, expanding what we mean by the comprehension of meaning "to include aesthetic response" (Galda 1988, 95).

Lee Galda observes that in addition to the reader and text, we must consider a third factor in any discussion of response to literature, and that is *context*. Readers read texts in particular contexts and as members of many different communities. Each of these communities influences how an individual responds to a particular book, as do other aspects of our personal experience and situation. (Remember the diversity of initial responses to the Jarrell poem among my students and me.) However, readers in a community do share—or come to share—a general agreement as to the meaning of a text. Meaning can be "*discussed* and *negotiated*" (Galda 1988, 95), as last summer we eventually decided together who and what "The Woman at the Washington Zoo" represents.

But while agreement on meaning can be reached, the significance of the literary work is another matter. In my own reading of "The Woman at the Washington Zoo," as a member of that class of forty-one, I was also a member of an exclusive community of two: Toby and me. The context for my reading of the poem included the fact that my husband chose it and the reasons that I imagined him choosing it. Once I knew, through my discussions with the group, that the speaker was a woman, a drab, low-level civil servant, and once I assumed that the poet was a man, probably of the Jarrell-Lowell-Berryman era because I know my husband's tastes, I was ready to really dislike this poem as condescending and sexist. Within this other, exclusive community of two, Toby and I talked about the poem in the context of a man's attempts to write from a woman's perspective, particularly Updike's latest novels, which neither of us has liked. Thus, the *significance* of the poem for me was much more individual. It would have been presumptuous beyond belief for me to go to class the next day and tell my forty students that each of them should respond to "The Woman at the Washington Zoo" as I had responded.

Anne and I know that *From Egg to Chick* is about a birth cycle, but as a member of a community of three-year-old girls, she responded to the fluffy chick. We agree that Cinderella is about a good person's dream coming true, but while I responded—badly—to Cinderella's passivity, Anne said she liked "when they get married and all the magic parts." It would be equally presumptuous for me to tell this much younger student how to read and react to her fairy tales.

Fairy tales are the most famous example of literature on which adults have attempted to impose meanings for children. In a recent study Ann Trousdale (1989) asked three eight-year-old girls "what meanings or morals the tales had for them" (37). Trousdale used "Snow White" and "The Sleeping Beauty," the Grimm versions and the Faerie Tale Theatre dramatizations (in which a moral is announced at the show's end), as well as the children's own telling of the stories. She found that the three girls "were actively engaged [in] making their own meanings of the tales, interpreting them in light of their own personal experiences, preoccupations, and inner needs. . . . They found moral lessons in the tales, but they were not the lessons which adults have claimed that the tales offered" (38).

For example, in *The Uses of Enchantment: The Meaning and Importance of Fairy Tales*, Bruno Bettelheim (1977) writes that the message of "Snow White" is a warning about the "evil consequences of narcissism for both parent and child" (203) and the need to control sexual jealousy. Faerie Tale Theatre draws a similar moral about the danger of vanity.

But to the three girls, the significance of the story was not the evil of vanity. None of them connected the Queen's narcissism with their own mothers or with themselves. It was the Queen's *cruelty* that two of the three found significant. The moral they drew was, roughly, "Don't do things to people; they might do things back."

As for "Sleeping Beauty," Bettelheim maintains that the prince's arrival "at the right time" is interpreted by children as "an event which causes sexual awakening"; the story further "impresses every child that a traumatic event—such as the girl's

bleeding at the beginning of puberty, and later, in first inter-
course—does have the happiest consequences" (234). Among
the three girls, one found no lesson, and one spoke again of
retribution ("Never to be mean . . . if you're mean you get
caught. . ."). The third was so familiar with the Faerie Tale Theatre version that she could recite their moral, about "good things
coming" when the time is right, right along with the narrator;
however, she, too, found her own lesson in "Sleeping Beauty":
"Don't make a fuss [if you don't get an invitation]. . . . If you
don't, just don't worry about it."

Trousdale concludes that at least on a conscious level "the
meanings and morals of the stories for the children were quite
different from the morals which adults found in the stories—
much more concrete, practical, and direct" (43). While Bettelheim suggests, rightly I think, that children use elements in the
tales to objectify inner conflicts, Trousdale points out that "it is
important to recognize that *what those conflicts will be* at a particular time will be highly individualized" (45).

Recent critics of the Grimm brothers have contended that
fairy tales represent less Bettleheim's universal and timeless
truths than a historical record of the values and anxieties of
particular times and places (Bottigheimer 1989). Sibling rivalry
in Cinderella may in fact reflect the very real struggle for food in
rural France in Medieval times, and the feasts and miraculous
animals in fairy tales may have been dreamed up by hungry
people—while we in the generations after Freud listen for mes-
sages to the psyche rather than comfort for the stomach. The
fairy tale is a screen on which changing wishes play. Rosenblatt
might add that all literature is such a screen onto which various
readers and communities of readers project our changing values.

Trousdale concludes about her three eight-year-olds:

[U]sing fairy tales to teach particular moral lessons is not
a wise practice either inside or outside the classroom.
Expecting children to derive particular morals from the
tales will prove likely to be an exercise in frustration and
confusion, for both children and adults. Opportunity to
reflect on the story and to come to some insight or conclusion is certainly beneficial, but it can be better done
in a forum which allows open-ended discussion. In such

a setting, children's attempts to bring a tale into personal significance may occur without fear of rejection or criticism. (45)

One issue for the teacher of literature is how to create such settings. If reader, text, and context all matter, how do we make sure that the classroom isn't a repressive context that dictates what and how children read and respond, denying the possibility of a live circuit between child and text?

First, I think that teachers need experience reading and discussing books—kids' books *and* adult literature—to help us distinguish between efferent and aesthetic responses to literature, between *reading activities* and *literary discussions*. What if my teacher friend who is having such a difficult time with literature became a reader too, not just of professional books, which she reads efferently in search of information about teaching and learning, but of novels, poetry, history, and essays, to which she might turn for the satisfactions of an aesthetic experience? When teachers read aesthetically, talk about our reading, and listen to how we talk, we discover the nature of literary conversation, of reader-to-reader talk. We break free of the old misconceptions of what reading is and how teachers are supposed to talk about it.

Genuine literary conversation does not take the form of stilted questions that we would be embarrassed to ask of another adult. It is informal, authentic, and opinionated. And it is comfortable. Donald Graves telephoned me recently for a bit of literary conversation, and it went something like this:

DON: Did you read the story by Lorrie Moore in the *New Yorker?*

NANCIE: Jesus, what a depressing story.

DON: The character is incredible. She sees irony everywhere, but nobody else sees it. Nobody knows her, not even her own sister.

NANCIE: I just sat there when I finished it. I mean, I was *numb* with depression. The difference between the person she is and the life she's having was unbearable. This gap—

DON: Gaps everywhere, between her and everyone. It's a tragedy. The taxi driver was the only honest person in her life. And that jerk on the balcony. All I can see is that stupid magic marker for the checks. And her *sister* set it up. It's grotesque—that end scene.

NANCIE: But the writing was so witty. So there's another gap— between loving the writing and the wit and being devastated by this person's life.

DON: Bonnie Sunstein gave me a call and told me I had to read it. Have you seen anything else by her?

NANCIE: Her name is familiar. I don't think I've seen it on a book.

DON: It makes you wonder how much of this is hers. . . .

NANCIE: Oh, God. It's too depressing to think about.

Our talk is personal, speculative, and gossipy. It's about our understanding of the story and our appreciation of the author's craft. And it is respectful. Don and I both know that neither of us will ask the other, "Where did the girl live? What was the significance of the taxi driver? What happened at the end of the story?" Teachers who know firsthand the pleasure of reading literature *relax.* They love reading, they trust that kids will find the same satisfaction in reading as they do, and they ask questions that go beyond what is in the text—but always come back to it.

These are the teachers who are seen by their students as readers, as people to whom students wish to apprentice themselves. In Durham, New Hampshire, the eighth-grade students of Linda Rief (1989) know that she is always ready to explore possibilities with books, that she will never work from old lesson plans or a teacher's manual, that she will read and write with them not so she can be a model for them but because reading and writing are what Linda does. A literature-based reading program works when it is founded on a teacher's immersion in literacy.

In literature-based reading we provide opportunities for wide reading. We set aside time in the classroom for students to be with books, to listen to works read aloud, and to respond independently. We introduce new authors, genres, texts, and styles of writing that we have encountered in our reading. And we accommodate young readers' choice of books. Only when children choose books do they get a full sense of what real readers do and what reading is good for. Their engagement with the books that they have selected promotes the development of personal tastes in literature, personal styles of reading, and personal styles of response. Literature-based reading requires active readers who have literacy preferences, just as a writer's workshop requires active writers with individual intentions and styles. Students who were raised on basals and anthologies will need help adjusting to a classroom where aesthetic response is the norm, where a teacher will ask them what they think about a literary work and why rather than requesting a plot synopsis or the main idea, just as kids raised on grammar worksheets and creative writing recipes need help adjusting to the autonomy and responsibility of a writing workshop.

One way that we help readers make the transition, in addition to our demonstrations as joyfully literate adults, is by providing opportunities for many different modes of response to literature: mini-lessons, small-group discussions, large-group share sessions, art, and drama. And we can ask for many different modes of written response to books: open-ended reading logs, prompted journal responses, dialogue journals with the teacher and peers, and multi-genre responses such as those written by Tom Romano's high school students, which feature student poems, songs, newspaper accounts, magazine feature articles, imitations, correspondence, and dramatic encounters—literature they have written in response to the literature they have read.

We also help readers through the ways that we respond to their responses. If our interpretations of a book, poem, or story differ from our students', or theirs from each other, we can ask *why*. We can explore the roots of our differences and make the reading richer (Galda 1988, 100). We can show students where our responses come from and encourage them to teach us and each other about why they feel and think as they do about the texts they read, to include comprehension as part of the aesthetic response.

I have learned that dialogue journals about literature are a particularly rich context for this kind of exploration—where teacher and student can level, reader to reader, and explore their responses in depth. Scott, an eighth grader, wouldn't acknowledge me when we passed in the hall and seldom volunteered to talk in class, but in the pages of his dialogue journal we discovered together what we thought about the novels of S. E. Hinton.

Ms. Atwell—

I finished *The Outsiders* today. That and *Big Red* are the *best* books I've ever read. I noticed she used *Outsiders* characters in *That Was Then*. It was neat. I liked it when they saved the kids from the burning church, and when Johny killed Bob because he was drowning Pony. I liked *all* of it. I felt sorry for Pony when Johny died. I was hoping he wouldn't die, so he could see more of the world. I liked the way she tells about Soda; kind of makes you idle him, huh? I also liked it when they were fighting, like when they beat the Socs. I think Hinton is an excellent author. I didn't know she was a girl until you told the whole class! That didn't bother me, though (that she's a *girl* author.) I might read *Tex* now. Do you know any more stories with violence, like gangs, and muggers and fights? I hope so, I kind of like them. Is there violence in *Tex*?

Scott

P. S. If you had the choice, whose side would you like to be on, the Socs or the Greasers? I would pick the Greasers because they're more like a family.

Dear Scott,

If I had to choose, given what Hinton shows us about the two groups, I'd be a Greaser. But to tell you the truth, I think she could have written this book from a Soc's point of view (maybe called it *The Insiders*), and readers would have loved the Soc gang. Here's my point: she takes us beyond outward appearances, into her characters' minds and hearts, and we can't help but care about them. She does it by telling thoughts and feelings—by having Pony tell us what he thinks and feels. It's pretty hard to hate someone when you really get close and come to know them. I think that's what she was trying to do—give us characters we normally wouldn't touch with ten-foot poles and make us stop judging books by their covers, stop putting down people we don't really know.

Keep in mind how knowing Pony's thoughts and feelings helped you as a reader. (It helps your readers, too.)

Have you read *The Contender* or *Durango Street?* I think they're just what you're looking for.

Ms. Atwell

Scott took his cues from me, as have the students of countless teachers across North America. These teachers' aesthetic orientation toward literature and encouragement of a diversity of opinions about the significance of texts invite children to respond aesthetically, too—to begin to make "true music" as co-authors of the works they read. Their classrooms are filled with literature, but in these classrooms the books need individual students to bring them to life and give them significance. The literature-based reading program is geared toward what children can bring to the books, not toward what they are supposed to get from the books. And because students bring to literature, they can take and take— joy, release, escape, enlightenment, rage, satisfaction, insight, relief, understanding, comfort.

Anne and I were reading Ruth Brown's version of *A Dark, Dark Tale* (1981). When we came to the last page, she noticed the look of terror on the face of the mouse as he cowers in the box that is his home. "He looks frightened," she said. "Why is he so scared, Mama?" I answered, "Maybe it's because two big people are staring down at him." She studied the illustration of the mouse's tiny home for another moment, then disagreed. "No, he's frightened because he doesn't have any books in there with him."

We cannot allow literature to be reduced to a method for transmitting so-called reading skills invented by textbook publishers. We must value literature, in Rosenblatt's words, "as a means of enlarging [our] knowledge of the world, because through literature [we] acquire not so much additional information as additional experience . . . literature provides a *living through*" (1938, 30). In the end, I hope that we will surround children with literature because we cherish it and them, and because literature will give them lives that we want them to know. The world is a frightening place. When we look beyond the basal, let it be toward the ways that literature might illumine our students' lives and make them whole.

"The end of reading is not more books but more life."

5 FINDING POETRY EVERYWHERE

J

UNE OAKES IS A BOOTHBAY GRANDMOTHER AND ONE OF MY DAUGH-
ter's oldest friends. She took care of Anne during her first few
months, when I returned to my classroom to finish out the
school year. One still, hot afternoon this past July the three of
us sat gossiping around her kitchen table. I was despairing over
Anne's refusal to accept that the summer sun could be bright
at bedtime, and June recited the first stanza of Robert Louis
Stevenson's "Bed in Summer":

> In winter I get up at night
> And dress by yellow candle-light.
> In summer, quite the other way,
> I have to go to bed by day.

I said, "I haven't thought of that poem in forever," and
June explained, "That was my primer, you know, when I was
a grammar school girl. I learned to read from the poems in *A
Child's Garden of Verses.*" I thought that it must have been a
sweet prescription.

The poet Karla Kuskin observed, "The French critic
Joseph Joubert once said, 'You will find poetry nowhere unless
you bring some of it with you.' To which might be added that
if you do bring some of it with you, you will find it everywhere." June has brought Robert Louis Stevenson's verse with
her for over sixty years. She found poetry in our kitchen conversation because poetry had been the written language of her
one-room schoolhouse.

This essay is about poetry—reading it, writing it, and how we might do a better job of teaching both. I'll begin by confessing my bias. I majored in English. I think that poetry is the ultimate genre to read and to write. I don't think that Somerset Maugham went nearly far enough when he effused:

> The crown of literature is poetry. It is its end and aim. It is the sublimest activity of the human mind. It is the achievement of beauty and delicacy. The writer of prose can only step aside when the poet passes.

For all my passion about poems I was, for years, the worst possible teacher of poetry. I barely taught it at all. When I did, it was in the form of line-by-line critical analysis or empty writing exercises. I was such a snob about the "crown of literature" that I didn't think that my kids were good enough for the poetry that I loved; I thought that what they needed was some watered-down school version from the Scott-Foresman anthology. My students never found poetry anywhere. Real poetry was for me, for the teacher's sublime mind.

Other teachers I knew didn't think that they were good enough for poetry. They avoided teaching it too, but because they were intimidated by it. They perceived poetry as difficult: difficult to read, difficult to understand, and, especially, difficult to talk about. They stopped reading it the moment it stopped being required. The junior year in college marked the end of their histories as readers of poetry—and what a relief. Never again to have to invent and support a thesis statement about a poem, never again to feel thick and incompetent in the company of English professors—and English majors—who rattled off "correct" interpretations, never again to have to understand that poetry was accessible only to the chosen few.

Thomas Newkirk has written about what he calls the "Pedagogy of Mystification that prevails in many literature classes": the method of critical analysis that hides the process of reading a poem and concentrates instead on products, on the professor's smooth, full-blown interpretation of the poem without ever revealing the real, messy business of how the professor got there (1990). When students don't have a sense of how a teacher gets there, of how a teacher reads a poem and grasps a meaning, it is unlikely that they will ever develop a sense of themselves as readers of poetry. Newkirk says that the result is "a pervasive lack of confidence when it comes to reading poetry." He sees "intelligent students, ones who could work late in the night to perfect computer programs, ones who could repair automobiles or who could make it down to Fort Lauderdale and back on fifty dollars, in short students who had shown over and over again that they could deal with difficulty. Yet they could be stopped by a poem." These are the students who stop poems just as soon as they can at the end of their junior year. Some become teachers—but not of poetry.

Sixty years ago, when June Oakes was a grammar school girl, fully half of the literature taught to fourth graders in the United States was poetry. Today, it's 97 percent prose and just 3 percent poetry. It would be easy to criticize the committees that compile basal readers for virtually ignoring poetry, among their other sins of omission and commission. But I think the problem cuts deeper, that it is more a matter of individual teachers' experiences with poetry. Either we read it and love it, as I did, but can't imagine how to begin to help children experience it fully and so end up lecturing about it or assigning cute formulas for our kids to write; or we don't read it and don't love it and relegate it to an enrichment unit that we'll assign in June if we don't run out of time.

Poetry deserves better, and children deserve better. I'm going to make my case for more poetry in three parts: first, reasons to read poetry and to write it; then, what poetry does (because it does much more than rhyme); and, finally, how we might invite kids to read and write it, some practical recommendations so that poetry can once again become one of the written languages of our classrooms.

In his essay "The Noble Rider and the Sound of Words," the poet Wallace Stevens writes that the poet's role "is to help people live their lives" (1951). Similarly, Marge Piercy speaks of her desire that her poems *work* for others. The title of one of her favorites of her poems is "To be of use." *Poetry* should be of use. Piercy writes:

> What I mean by useful is simply that readers will find poems that speak to and for them, will take those poems into their lives and say them to each other and put them up on the bathroom wall and remember bits and pieces of

them in stressful or quiet moments. That the poems may give voice to something in the experience of a life has been my intention. To find ourselves spoken for in art gives dignity to our pain, our anger, our lust, our losses. We can hear what we hope for and what we most fear, in the small release of cadenced utterance. We have few rituals that function for us in the ordinary chaos of our lives. (1982, xii)

My public school education was not rich in poetry—my love of poems came later, through my wonderfully literate husband— but two poems are the memorable pieces of literature of my adolescence. In 1968 or 1969, *Life* magazine articles about the Vietnam war and U. S. race relations featured two poems as sidebars. One was "What Were They Like?", a poem by Denise Levertov about the Vietnamese people, which was written as a series of questions that an anthropologist might ask about a vanished race. The other was "What happens to a dream deferred?" by Langston Hughes. I carried these scraps of poetry with me through twenty years of moves, they meant so much to me, struck so deep with me. My anguish over the state of my country—its foreign policy and its policies at home—was spoken for in the poems. They were rituals that functioned for me in my ordinary life, talismans clipped from *Life* magazine that gave me a glimpse of how poetry could work for people. When I finally became a teacher of poetry, I saw eighth graders take poems into their lives in the same way—not the dusty chestnuts from the Scott-Foresman anthology, but contemporary poetry that gave voice to something in their experience: Robert Frost's "Nothing Gold Can Stay," Elizabeth Bishop's "Fishing," "Foul Shot" by Edwin Hoey, "anyone lived in a pretty how town" by e e cummings.

We can't risk the chance that students will stumble across e e cummings. We must bring poetry into our classrooms. Lee Bennett Hopkins has written that poetry is a source of love and hope that children carry with them the rest of their lives, that it opens up a world of feelings for children that they never thought possible. It is also literature that can work with any grade, any age, and meet the interests and abilities of anyone, anywhere, from the most gifted to the most reluctant reader (1987). And it is literature that can be about any subject and any theme. When I finally began to teach poetry in my classroom, I watched my students realize that poetic topics were not limited to love, despair, roses, and rainbows. Poetry could be about anything.

"YOU CAN'T WRITE A POEM ABOUT MCDONALD'S"

Noon. Hunger the only thing
singing in my belly.
I walk through the blossoming cherry trees
on the library mall,
past the young couples coupling,
by the crazy fanatic
screaming doom and salvation
at a sensation-hungry crowd,
to the Lake Street McDonald's.
It is crowded, the lines long and sluggish.
I wait in the greasy air.
All around me people are eating—
the sizzle of conversation,
the salty odor of sweat,
the warm flesh pressing out of
hip huggers and halter tops.
When I finally reach the cash register,
the counter girl is crisp as a pickle,
her fingers thin as french fries,
her face brown as a bun.
Suddenly I understand cannabalism.
As I reach for her,
she breaks into pieces
wrapped neat and packaged for take-out.
I'm thinking, how amazing it is
to live in this country, how easy
it is to be filled.
We leave together, her warm aroma
close at my side.
I walk back through the cherry trees
blossoming up into pies,
the young couples frying in
the hot, oily sun,

the crowd eating up the fanatic,
singing, my ear, eye, and tongue
fat with the wonder
of this hungry world.

RONALD WALLACE

MAYBE DATS YOUWR PWOBLEM TOO

All my pwoblems
who knows, maybe evwybody's pwoblems
is due to da fact, due to da awful twuth
dat I am SPIDERMAN.

I know, I know. All da dumb jokes:
No flies on you, ha ha,
and da ones about what do I do wit all
doze extwa legs in bed. Well, dat's funny yeah.
But you twy being
SPIDERMAN for a month or two. Go ahead.

You get doze cwazy calls fwom da
Gubbener askin you to twap some booglar who's
only twying to wip off color T. V. sets.
Now, what do I cawre about T. V. sets?
But I pull on da suit, da stinkin suit,
wit da sucker cups on da fingers,
and get my wopes and wittle bundle of
equipment and den I go flying like cwazy
acwoss da town fwom woof top to woof top.

Till der he is, some poor dumb color T. V. slob
and I fall on him and we westle a widdle
until I get him all woped. So big deal.

You tink when you SPIDERMAN
der's sometin big going to happen to you.
Well, I tell you what. It don't happen dat way.
Nuttin happens. Gubbener calls, I go.
Bwing him to powice. Gubbener calls again,
like dat over and over.

I tink I twy sometin diffunt. I tink I twy
sometin excitin like wacing cawrs. Sometin to make

my heart beat at a difwent wate.
But den you just can't quit being sometin like
SPIDERMAN.
You SPIDERMAN for life. Fowever. I can't even
buin my suit. It won't buin. It's fwame wesistent.
So maybe dat's youwr pwoblem too, who knows.
So maybe dat's da whole pwoblem wif evwytin.
Nobody can buin der suits, day all fwame wesistent.
Who knows?

JIM HALL

My students were even more surprised to discover that poetry does not have to rhyme. Poets do play with rhyme, but they also play with form, sound, and language, with feelings and symbols and images. Poets play with the rules and bend them to suit their subjects and themselves. Nikki Giovanni plays with punctuation—or, rather, she plays without it in her poem about a big brother.

STARS

in science today we learned
that stars are a mass of gases that burned
out a long time ago only we don't know
that because we still see the glow

and i remembered my big brother Donny
said he burned out a long time ago and i asked
him did that make him
a star

Robert Francis plays with rhythm and repetition in "While I Slept," a poem about a mother.

WHILE I SLEPT

While I slept, while I slept and the night grew colder
She would come to my room, stepping softly
And draw a blanket about my shoulder
While I slept.

While I slept, while I slept in the dark, still heat
She would come to my bedside, stepping coolly
And smooth the twisted, troubled sheet
While I slept.

Now she sleeps, sleeps under quiet rain
While nights grow warm or nights grow colder.
And I wake, and sleep, and wake again
While she sleeps.

And Ted Kooser plays with metaphor: to a child, the thunder is a bird of prey.

CHILD FRIGHTENED BY A THUNDERSTORM

Thunder has nested in the grass all night
and rumpled it, and with its outstretched wings
has crushed the peonies. Its beak was bright,
sharper than garden shears and, clattering,
it snipped bouquets of branches for its bed.
I could not sleep. The thunder's eyes were red.

What else does poetry do? Like a telegram, it doesn't waste words. It conveys the essence of the thing. The poet William Cole has said that poetry is "beautiful shorthand." In this miniature, the power lies in the economy of its language.

THE MILL BACK HOME

Logs drowse in the pond
Dreaming of their heroes
Alligator and crocodile
                    VERN RUTSALA

Poetry can comment on literature itself, giving us a new perspective on familiar tales and characters. When I read William Steig's *Sylvester and the Magic Pebble* (1969), in which poor Sylvester becomes trapped inside a rock, to grade school children, I also share Charles Simic's "Stone" to make the reading richer and even more mysterious.

STONE

Go inside a stone
That would be my way.
Let somebody else become a dove
Or gnash with a tiger's tooth.
I am happy to be a stone.

From the outside the stone is a riddle:
No one knows how to answer it.
Yet within, it must be cool and quiet
Even though a cow steps on it full weight.
Even though a child throws it in a river;
The stone sinks, slow, unperturbed
To the river bottom
Where the fishes come to knock on it
And listen.

I have seen sparks fly out
When two stones are rubbed,
So perhaps it is not dark inside after all;
Perhaps there is a moon shining
From somewhere, as though behind a hill—
Just enough light to make out
The strange writings, the star-charts
On the inner walls.

Poetry also makes us laugh; it tickles us. Jack Prelutsky and
Shel Silverstein are perhaps this country's greatest ambassadors of
poetry because of their direct, contemporary language, because
of their topics, which all children can see eye-to-eye with, and
because their poems are funny and make the reading of poetry
fun. Another whose nonsense verse makes children laugh is
Dennis Lee.

THE PUZZLE

Annie and Ernie
  McGilligan Spock
Pedalled their tricycles
  Round the block.

They pedalled and pedalled
  And pedalled in pairs,
Till they came to a house
  That was just like theirs.

In the same front yard
  Stood the same small tree;
On the same brown table
  The same pot of tea;

And the very same smells!
  And the very same noise!
And the very same beds
  With the very same toys!

They stood and they stared
  And they stared and they stood;
The thing was too weird
  To be understood:

How was it possible?
  Think of the shock
Of Annie and Ernie
  McGilligan Spock!

DENNIS LEE

And poems shape and share more serious feelings. Donald Murray writes "Poets remind us not to preach, but merely to reveal" (1986). For me the best writing about the war in Vietnam was not an essay or speech but a collection of verse by Michael Casey. The best writing about emotional illness is the poetry of Anne Sexton; the best writing about personal relationships is the poetry of Sharon Olds; the best writing about relationships between people and the natural world is by Mary Oliver and Robert Frost. These writers never preach. They open up the world of feelings by showing it to us rather than telling us about it. In his poem "Incident" Countee Cullen *reveals* racism through a child's response to a racial epithet.

INCIDENT

Once riding in old Baltimore,
  Heart-filled, head-filled with glee,
I saw a Baltimorean
  Keep looking straight at me.

Now I was eight and very small,
   And he was no whit bigger,
And so I smiled, but he poked out
   His tongue, and called me, "Nigger."

I saw the whole of Baltimore
   From May until December;
Of all the things that happened there
   That's all that I remember.

Marge Piercy *reveals* a woman's response to what some have
defined as a woman's role.

WHAT'S THAT SMELL
IN THE KITCHEN?

All over America women are burning dinners.
It's lambchops in Peoria; it's haddock
in Providence; it's steak in Chicago
tofu delight in Big Sur; red
rice and beans in Dallas.
All over America women are burning
food they're supposed to bring with calico
smile on platters glittering like wax.
Anger sputters in her brainpan, confined
but spewing out missiles of hot fat.
Carbonized despair presses like a clinker
from a barbeque against the back of her eyes.
If she wants to grill anything, it's
her husband spitted over a slow fire.
If she wants to serve him anything
it's a dead rat with a bomb in its belly
ticking like the heart of an insomniac.
Her life is cooked and digested,
nothing but leftovers in Tupperware.
Look, she says, once I was roast duck
on your platter with parsley but now I am Spam.
Burning dinner is not incompetence but war.

As a mother of a young child, I am just discovering something else that poetry does. It is teaching my daughter how to
read. The predictability of rhymed or rhythmic verse and the

repetition in many poems support her as she begins to match the words she has heard in a hundred read-alouds to their configurations on the page. Liz Cornell teaches reading to her first graders through poetry (1987). She and her students demonstrate the power of singing and chorally reading poetry in a classroom that is filled with verse, from charts and posters to Mother Goose, big books, and *Poems Children Will Sit Still For,* newly released as *Sing a Song of Popcorn* (de Regniers, Moore, White, and Carr 1988). *Sing a Song of Popcorn* is my daughter's favorite anthology of poetry. Imagine her chubby finger touching all the *Yeses* when we read "My Favorite Word."

MY FAVORITE WORD

There is one word—
My favorite—
The very, very best.
It isn't No or Maybe.
It's Yes, Yes, Yes, *Yes,* YES.

"Yes, yes, you may," and
"Yes, of course," and
"Yes, please help yourself."
And when I want a piece of cake,
"Why, yes. It's on the shelf."

Some candy? "Yes."
A cookie? "Yes."
A movie? "Yes, we'll go."

I love it when they say my word:
Yes, *Yes,* YES! (*Not No.*)
LUCIA AND JAMES L. HYMES, JR.

To get ready to write this essay about poetry, I read poetry. As I read, I flagged the poems that I might include. I marked poems that I liked and thought that others might, and poems that showed what poems can do. It was the requisite preparation for writing about poetry, and it is also the requisite preparation for the teacher who wishes to begin teaching poetry. Read it. Read it and be amazed at what contemporary poetry does. This is the poetry that we never got to in high school or college because we were so busy covering "The Wreck of the Hesperus." Read it and understand how contemporary poetry means. Read it for yourself first, to fall in love with it. Mark the poems that you love to share with your students.

Teachers new to poetry, or intimidated by it, might want to start with *Writing Poems* by Robert Wallace (1987), which is both an anthology of great poetry and a text for writing poetry of one's own. Wallace is also a poet, and *Writing Poems* is clear, forthright, and inviting. A similar book, written for eight- to twelve-year-old children, is *Knock at a Star: A Child's Introduction to Poetry* by X. J. and Dorothy Kennedy (1982). The Kennedys combine superb poetry with down-to-earth advice about reading it. And I especially recommend a book by the poet and teacher Georgia Heard, *For the Good of the Earth and Sun* (1989).

There are many fine anthologies of poetry for children available today and many poets writing well for children, but I think some books are essentials for the classroom library: the gorgeous collection *Talking to the Sun* (1985), edited by Kenneth Koch and Kate Farrell; *Sing a Song of Popcorn* (1988), an anthology illustrated by nine Caldecott Medalists; for adolescents, Cynthia Rylant's *Waiting to Waltz* (1984) and *The Soda Jerk* (1990) and any of the anthologies edited by Paul Janeczko; the holiday, seasonal, and animal anthologies of Lee Bennett Hopkins and Myra Cohn Livingston; *A Child's Calendar* by John Updike (1965); Eloise Greenfield's *Honey I Love and Other Poems* (1978); and anything by David McCord, Arnold Adoff, Karla Kuskin, and Valerie Worth.

One impediment to the reading of poetry is that it is not easy to spot in school and public libraries. Poetry is buried in the 800's, far away from the storybooks and novels that are our more accustomed sources of pleasure reading. When I tracked down the poetry shelves in the Boothbay Region Elementary School library, after teaching at the school for almost ten years, I discovered a treasure trove of books for me to read to myself, and then to my kids, and then for my kids to read to themselves.

When I began to teach poetry, I collected copies of the poems that I liked, filled a folder with them, and shared my favorites with my students. I only read aloud poems that I liked, so that my invitation to kids to become readers and lovers of poetry would be as genuine as I could make it. I read poetry in mini-lessons in both writing and reading workshop, and sometimes I read a poem before the mini-lesson or at the end of the workshop.

After a few bungled readings I learned never to read a poem cold. I practiced—and marked my copy for pauses and stresses—so that my voice could give meaning to the poem, could share the poet's feelings, and could mediate the poem for my students. I tried to read in a normal voice, following the rhythm of the poem but naturally, as though I were telling the kids about a new car or a TV program (Hopkins 1987). And I learned to devise ways to show my kids the poems that they were hearing. In a genre in which form and content are equally important, kids need to know what poetry looks like, to see how a poet uses the white space on the page to create rhyme, rhythm, emphasis, deemphasis, shape, pauses, and stops. So I made individual copies of the poetry I read, or wrote poems on the board or on chart paper, or projected them on overhead transparencies. And as kids followed along, they could see how I used my voice to make my own sense of the poem.

Remembering Newkirk's Pedagogy of Mystification, I made sure that students knew that these performances were not my first readings, and I often described the problems I'd had deciding how to read a poem. I also told them why I had chosen to read a poem—what in the work had spoken to me. I pointed out things I had noticed about the poem on my first and second and third and fourth readings. Most importantly, I asked them what they thought of the poem and why, or what they had noticed about how it was written. I learned to de-mystify the process of reading a poem so that my students might see how a reader could relish unraveling the difficulties of poetry. And I learned about the difference between talking a poem to death and, instead, inviting readers to see how it works. I avoided line-by-line analysis, finding the main idea and supporting details, and those inane "creative" responses: What color is this poem? What animal does this poem remind you of? Can you draw this poem?

Sometimes, with such short, memorable poems as Frost's "The Pasture" or "Dust of Snow," I asked students to say them with me several times in a choral reading. I didn't require memorization, since some kids simply can't do it, but I did encourage it. As the Kennedys observe in *Knock at a Star*, in the course of a happy, successful choral reading, "memorization isn't a chore, but one more way of reminding children that poems aren't merely to be seen, but also to be heard, and kept" (1982, 134)—and taken with them, so that children may find these poems again in a real pasture spring, in a real dust of snow.

As often as not, I didn't talk about the poems I read aloud to my classes. Some days after I read we all just sat quietly for a minute and savored the poem before moving on to our other business as writers and readers. Teachers who have avoided poetry because they don't feel comfortable talking about it can find poems that they like and simply share the magic with children: read a poem and then be quiet. By itself this is more than a generous bequest to a group of children.

In addition to reading poetry aloud, we can talk about poetry in mini-lessons. Teachers can use examples of poems as I've done here to show what poetry does and to teach (illustrating with appropriate poems) some of the technical language of poets: simile and metaphor, alliteration, rhyme and rhythm, blank verse, rhyme scheme, persona, stanza, and line break. *Writing Poems* (Wallace 1987) and *For the Good of the Earth and Sun* (Heard 1989) are especially helpful for a teacher who wishes to develop a vocabulary for talking about poetry.

As Marna Bunce (1989) has suggested, we can also find poetry in prose. We can look for and talk about prose language that is particularly imageful or rhythmic, as in *Owl Moon* by Jane Yolen, *I'm in Charge of Celebrations* by Byrd Baylor, or Cynthia Rylant's *When I Was Young in the Mountains*. Marna's students copied examples of beautiful language that they came across in their reading into individual notebooks, which served as a poetry thesaurus for their own writing. Another possibility is a bulletin board that students fill with nuggets of beautiful language that they find in prose and poetry.

I began to cover the bulletin boards, walls, and doors of my classroom with poetry. I took down the Argus posters, copied out great, short poems, taped them up, and invited my kids to do the same. Sometimes we masked rhyming words with post-it notes so readers might predict the rhymes underneath. And when students began to write poetry of their own, one option for publishing it was to create a new poetry poster for the classroom. Their poetry was also published in individual bound books, in class magazines, on dittoes, and in the school's literary paper. As with any other genre, my students wrote poetry in order for it to be read. And I began to highlight students' poetry in mini-lessons, to read aloud and share how I read Alice Gilchrist's and Tim McGrath's poems with the same attention as I discussed Emily Dickinson and Theodore Roethke.

For much too long I assumed that my students wouldn't write poetry unless I assigned it. Even after I transformed my English class into a writing workshop, I continued to call a halt to the workshop every few weeks to assign a poem. I thought poetry would not get written unless I required it, and I thought it would be poor poetry unless I provided a formula. In short, I continued to be a snob about poetry. I gave students the traditional school forms—couplets, limericks, cinquains, acrostics, and haikus—and also some kiddie varieties I'd uncovered on my own: five senses poems and who-what-when-where-why poems. *Wishes, Lies and Dreams* (Koch 1970) was my bible. My students wrote wish poems, lie poems, and color poems. They wrote comparisons, "If I Were the Snow" poems, and "I Seem to Be/But Really I Am" poems. They even wrote sestinas, an obscure seven-stanza form in which the poet uses the same six end words in various prescribed orders in each of the stanzas. In *Wishes, Lies and Dreams*, Kenneth Koch urges teachers to "invent forms in which certain words are given beforehand and the rest is left for children to fill in" (223). A semi-sestina by the poet Bruce Bennett illustrates the problem of approaching the writing of poetry as a fill-in-the-blank exercise. (Bennett's six words were *sestina, coffee, challenge, form, it,* and *promise.*)

SORT OF A SESTINA

IN PARTIAL FULFILLMENT OF THE REQUIREMENTS

"What? You've never written a sestina?"
You gazed incredulous across your coffee.
"But I should think you'd take it as a challenge;
I mean, with all your fancy-work in form.
Well, if you ever write one, let me see it."
"I will," I promised. Here. I've kept my promise.

The thing is, I don't write things for the challenge.
Of course, when something's done I like to see it,
And once I start, it's sort of like a promise:
For instance, if I said, "We'll meet for coffee,"
We'd meet for coffee. It's like that with form.
And that's the way it is with this "sestina."

Don't get me wrong. I love to play with form,
And there's a certain pleasure in a challenge.
Again for instance, I've included "coffee,"
A word that doesn't have a lot of promise,
To say the least, for use in a sestina.
Once having used it, I'm obliged to see it

Through. Okay. Let's say I'm stuck with "coffee."
I need a spot to stick it, then I see it
And bang! (as right above) I've met that challenge.
That's what you've got to do with a sestina.
You pounce on any opening with promise
And score your piddling points against the form.

But having seized those openings with promise
And being well along in one's sestina
And every time it comes around to coffee
Sneaking another by to beat the form
's not such a grand achievement, as I see it.
Suppose you prove you're equal to the challenge—

The point is, what's the point? Who's going to see it
As anything but diddling with a form?
That's *why* I've never written a sestina.
It's always seemed a wholly senseless challenge.
But I remembered what you said at coffee;
And also, since a promise is a promise

(Even when it takes form as a sestina),
I'm hoping you may see it as a challenge
To promise we will meet again for coffee.

I think that when we emphasize form in the writing of poetry by assigning formulas, we do so at the expense of meaning. We turn poetry into an exercise of getting the form to come out right. Denise Levertov has stated, "Form is never more than a revelation of content." Poetic forms should be introduced, but as means to serve individual students' needs as poets. There is no lovelier way to invite a sestina than to share Elizabeth Bishop's "Sestina" about a grandmother and her grandchild.

I finally stopped assigning poetry in writing workshop when I changed my reading program to a reading workshop. I shelved the class sets of anthologies and made time for students to read and talk with me and others about books that they had chosen. I began to read poetry aloud and to talk about it, and they began to read it and talk about it—and to write it. In this atmosphere, poetry was abundant and alive. The poet Donald Hall has written, "Our sense of the form of the poem—that resolution of rhythm, image, and feeling—lies deep inside us, but it comes from our reading, in which we develop our changing sense of what a good poem is, and from our revising toward that goal." My students became poets, but first they became readers of poetry.

Jack Wilde, a fifth-grade teacher, has said that we need to treat poetry "like architecture; we've got to let kids get inside of it and walk around for a while" (1989, 47). None of the student poems that I included in *In the Middle* grew from assignments. The poems evolved from kids getting inside poetry—reading it and talking about it. The poems evolved from real needs, real subjects that kids wanted to explore, and only this genre could do it. Dylan Thomas once said, "I've been a poet long enough to know you have to be urged from inside. You don't write a poem until there's a poem to write. And almost any poem is fifty to a hundred revisions." And my students' poems, too, evolved from hard work. There is a myth about writing poetry, that it is an exquisite experience that comes on the wings of a dove and requires kid glove response from the teacher. *Good* poetry is hard to write.

Kelli knows it. As an eighth-grade poet, she wrote about, as she put it, "the torment of adolescence." Figure 5–1 shows her first draft. Kelli acknowledged her debt to Robert Frost. He wants to be versed in country things; she wants to be versed in life.

In her second draft, Kelli began to play with the white space on the page (Figure 5–2). What happens if "My youth" gets a line of its own? What is the emphasis if "Problems" is a line all by itself? And what is conveyed if she makes the word *life* a proper noun?

In a third draft, Kelli experimented with stanzas (Figure 5–3). What happens if the word "Problems" is now a stanza of its own?

And finally, she recalled some of the shape poetry we had read in class. In her last draft (Figure 5–4) her youth literally *makes the bars.*

Kelli revised toward her sense of what a good poem is. By the end of April she carried inside her a wealth of experiences with

FIGURE 5–1

Kelli's First Draft

Trapped
My youth makes the bars that
  imprison me.
Being #̶, a teen, not knowing a thing,
  puts me behind those bars.
Problems - Always with no obrious
  ~~answer~~ solution,
Cause my confusion and eagerness
  to ~~a~~ be versed in life,
But those are the problems
  that solve ~~those~~ to come.

FIGURE 5–2

Kelli's Second Draft

Trapped
My youth
Makes the bars
That imprison me.
Being a teen -
Not knowing a thing
Puts me behind those bars.
Problems -
Always with no obvious solution,
Cause my confusion
And eagerness to be
Versed in life,
But those are the problems
That solve those to come.

► FIGURE 5–3 ◄

Kelli's Third Draft

Trapped
My youth
Makes the bars
That imprison me.

Being a teen
Not knowing a thing,
Puts me behind those bars.

Problems

Always with no obvious solution,
Cause my confusion
And eagerness to be versed
In Life.

But those are the problems
That solve
Those to come.

FIGURE 5–1

Kelli's Last Draft

Trapped

My Youth
M   T   B
a   h   a
k   e   r
e   s
s

That imprison me.

Being a teen
Not knowing a thing
Puts me behind those bars.

Problems —

Always with no obrious solutions—
Cause my confusion
And eagerness to be versed
In life.

But those are the problems
That solve
Those to come.

good poetry and a wealth of connections between poetry and her life. Poetry is useful to Kelli.

One afternoon my daughter and I took our favorite woods walk, along the Salt Pond Road to the beach at Hendricks Head. She has covered this half-mile a hundred times in her life, first in a Snugli, then in a stroller, then on her own strong legs. From the start I brought poetry with us, reciting to her for the length of our walk—"The Song of Hiawatha," "The Parade," "Alligator Pie," a half-dozen poems by Robert Frost. On this day we noticed that someone had thinned saplings and cleared the scrub and brush between the road and the Sheepscot River so that we could see the river deep through the trees. I said, "I wonder who owns this land." Anne's response was a poem:

Whose woods these are I think I know.
His house is in the village though;
He will not see me stopping here
To watch his woods fill up with snow.

My little horse must think it queer
To stop without a farmhouse near
Between the woods and frozen lake
The darkest evening of the year.

He gives his harness bells a shake
To ask if there is some mistake.
The only other sound's the sweep
Of easy wind and downy flake.

The woods are lovely, dark and deep
But I have promises to keep,
And miles to go before I sleep,
And miles to go before I sleep.

For me this single moment was reward enough for years of reading and living with poetry. The joy of it is that I know it is not an isolated moment. Anne will live other poems with me and without me. Poetry won't keep her safe. It won't ensure her a happy life or heal her pain or make her rich. But it will give voice to the experiences of her life. This seems enough to ask of it.

" 'You will find poetry nowhere unless you bring some of it with you.' To which might be added that if you do bring some of it with you, you will find it everywhere."

6

WHEN WRITING WORKSHOP WORKS

WHEN I SHELVED MY ENGLISH CURRICULUM IN ORDER TO become a teacher of writing, I began to call my classroom a writing workshop. I hoped that *workshop* would convey my intention to establish a place where students would behave like writers, where they would have time, choices, and access to others' responses, just like real writers, and where they could apprentice themselves to an adult practitioner of the craft of writing—namely me, their teacher.

Since the publication of *In the Middle,* I've read about and observed all manner of writing workshops, and usually I can recognize the trappings of the methods that I described in the book. Students are given regular time for writing. They choose their own topics and genres, and they confer with each other and the teacher about drafts in progress. The disheartening news is that some of the classrooms are no more workshops than the room down the hall where the kids are still studying *Warriner's.*

The affect is flat and the students are listless. Kids churn out "pieces" that go directly into file folders, never to be seen again. The range of genre is narrow, mostly narratives of personal experience. Worst of all, the quality of the writing is mediocre. The heart and the art of a workshop environment are missing.

Happily, I also visit and read about workshops where students are joyful, eloquent, obsessed writers. The variation among these classrooms is extraordinary. They range from

103

grade one to university, from rural to inner city, from factory public to private elite. But in every one of the effective workshops there is a constant: the teacher is acting like someone to whom students would wish to apprentice themselves. The teacher demonstrates what it means to be immersed in literacy and invites students to share a rich, compelling vision of the power of writing and reading. The heart and the art of good teaching are alive here.

I understand now that *In the Middle* can be read as a cookbook. By providing all the ingredients, I encouraged the misapprehension that a teacher could simply follow my recipe and produce readers and writers as avid and thoughtful as the students in my book. In concentrating on the story of my teaching and the methods I developed, I did not reflect sufficiently on who I had become in that classroom. And so I think it may be useful to consider the characteristics of the teachers whose workshops work for young writers—to consider how they have gone beyond traditional notions of method and to reflect on who they are to their students and what they do to sow the seeds of enthusiasm and excellence.

First and foremost, they are writers and readers. Because they write and read *for themselves,* the teachers know how accessible and satisfying writing and reading can be. They also know that they will write and read for a lifetime—not just during a summer institute or to model an annual example of "the writing process" for their kids—and so they relax. The pressure is off because they recognize that there will be many opportunities to succeed or fail at literacy, many opportunities to demonstrate everyday literacy to their kids.

The teachers are not writing the Great American Novel. When they write, it's to draft the new student handbook, plan a presentation for open house, complain to mail order companies, protest to the editor of the local newspaper, capture a precious time in their lives, describe observations of their kids and classrooms, compose memos to parents, respond in dialogue journals, keep in touch with distant family and friends, and tell others that they love them. They know that writing is not a single activity, and their students hear their many voices as writers. On overhead transparencies and in conferences, the teachers show students how they go about the various writing tasks that they use to make sense of their lives.

Most importantly, the teachers who write for themselves reject, finally and forever, what I have come to think of as The Bogus Tradition. They stop talking about such bogus English teacher concepts as topic sentences, the seven models of paragraph development, five-paragraph themes, outlining, compare/contrast essays, sensory details, and parts of speech. The advice that they give their students about genre, convention, and craft is based in reality. It comes from their own successful (and not so successful) experiences as writers and from reading good, honest writing about writing.

In workshops that work, the teacher has read such books as Donald Murray's *A Writer Teaches Writing* (1985) and *Write to Learn* (1990); William Zinsser's *On Writing Well* (1990) and *Inventing the Truth* (1987); and two books about the writing of poetry, *Writing Poems* by Robert Wallace (1987) and *For the Good of the Earth and Sun* by Georgia Heard (1989). They have drawn on such resources as *How Writers Write* by Pamela Lloyd (1987) and *Writers at Work: The Paris Review Interviews*. In these books professional novelists, poets, essayists, and journalists talk frankly about their craft and demonstrate how they go about it, as opposed to commercial materials that are compiled not by authors but by marketing experts invested in perpetuating The Bogus Tradition.

In workshops that work, teachers read for their own pleasure. They read novels, poetry, plays, adult and children's literature, books by their favorite authors, books their friends and colleagues recommend, books their students recommend. The teachers talk about what they read, how they read, and why they respond as they do, and they encourage—and accept—their students' tastes and responses. Kids know them as adults who read themselves to sleep at night.

In workshops that work, teachers read contemporary criticism and reviews. They know how literary critics write about books, and they recognize that this colloquial, often humorous, often first-person chat has nothing in common with the essay form that has been deified by The Bogus Tradition. There is not a five-paragraph theme to be found in *The New York Times Book Review*, but it is a practical, generous invitation to understanding how people in this country really write and talk about literature.

And in workshops that work, teachers read about ideas. They buy a reputable daily newspaper and turn to the op-ed page to learn how others are writing about the ideas of our times. They read Tom Wicker, Anthony Lewis, Mary McGrory, Ellen Goodman, Russell Baker. On occasion they bypass *Time* and *Newsweek* in favor of *The Nation* or *In These Times*. They understand that a citizenry is aliterate unless it uses literacy to consider the world. When they share political essays, commentaries, and reportage with their classes, they invite every student to become, in the poet Cavafy's words, "a member of the city of ideas."

In *Discover Your Own Literacy* (1990), Donald Graves describes a teacher's own reading and writing "as the base from which good teaching comes." He filled the book with practical invitations to teachers who wish to experiment with and reflect on their literacy. Graves identifies the best writing teachers as those who ask big questions and deal with them honestly, as those who make big decisions about their own literacy and expect students to do the same.

It is easy to lose sight of the big questions and the big decisions when confronted with the realities of public education: teaching loads of 125 students a day, low-tracked groupings in which the students never have opportunities to collaborate with kids who are good at reading and writing, classrooms in which only a handful of the kids speak English as a first language, schools where just gathering a sufficient quantity of paper and pens each day is a heroic gesture.

And it is easy to lose sight of the big questions and the big decisions when confronted with the public's attitude toward us and toward our kids—when the Education President proposes an education budget that barely keeps pace with inflation, when the Education Summit doesn't invite a single classroom teacher, when Tracy Kidder's best-seller (1989) about a teacher describes an empty, pre-fab curriculum, blames the students' disaffection and failure on the poverty of their families, and then is heralded as a study of a model educator—and not one of the reviewers is a teacher.

But if we ever hope to counter the realities of teaching, the first step is to ask the big questions. The next step is to make some big decisions about how we and our students might engage in the most powerful political acts of all, reading and writing.

In Newcastle, Maine, Judith Stafford despaired over her high school's system of tracking students for English. She wrote an article for the Maine English Council's journal about the dilemma of trying to teach process writing and literary response to groups of general students. Her writing sparked a collaboration with her colleague Kate Pennington in which an academic and a general class began to meet together every day as one class, which has led them to conduct a case study of the issues involved in heterogeneous grouping in the secondary English program.

Wheelwright, Kentucky, was once a mining town. Now its citizens are mostly retired miners, an older population that normally might not be interested in supporting education. At Wheelwright High School, Carol Stumbo and her students publish a magazine called *Mantrip*: a mantrip is the car that carries miners back into the mines. The magazine explores what technology does to people's values through interviews that Carol and her students conduct in their community, and she and the kids gather the community together at the school to celebrate the issues of the magazine.

In Washington, D.C., where the immigrant population has increased by over seventy percent in the last five years, community service, education, and mental health professionals have collaborated on The Books Project. In writing workshops in the D.C. public schools, Spanish-speaking children write, illustrate, and publish stories and instructional texts for the schoolchildren of Central America. Last summer Deborah Menkart, one of the project directors from George Washington University, delivered over a hundred colorful, handmade books to schools in El Salvador that have no books, no paper, no chalk or crayons. The Books Project also works at an immigrant high school in Washington, helping students from Central America tell the sagas of their journey to this country, and they are training Spanish-speaking junior high students to tutor elementary school children in writing.

Last fall, students and teachers from West Nyack, New York; Raleigh, North Carolina; Alanson, Michigan; Berea, Kentucky; and Lima, Peru, were among those who participated in an international discussion of the environmental crisis. Their conversation was written on computers and sponsored by Bread Net, the Bread Loaf computer network directed by Bill Wright. All of the students and teachers read and commented on a recent cover story from *Newsweek*. Then they generated questions about global environmental issues for The Nature Conservancy and for their own interview with Senator Albert Gore. Among other issues, they wanted to know:

- What is being done in the United States to prevent the destruction of the ozone layer?
- Is there federal support for recycling programs? If not, why not?
- Why does the EPA have to have such perfect scientific evidence to convict companies of environmental crimes? Why is there no law to prevent this from delaying court battles?
- Are there any international organizations formed or being formed to control pollution worldwide?

Then groups of students and teachers wrote about threats to the environment in their immediate areas and submitted commentaries to an international electronic essay exchange.

In Winnipeg, Manitoba, Syd Korsunsky had been teaching English for sixteen years. Last year, in their first writing workshop, he and his ninth graders discovered what writing is good for. In a letter he wrote to me, Syd has come alive with the possibilities of his junior high kids as they use the workshop to ask the big questions.

Dear Ms. Atwell:

In one short month my kids have already blown me away with their own topics, things like: a 15-year retrospective on Chile from a student who longs to return to her homeland; a wistful "homesick" piece by a student from Korea who saw the Olympics on TV and realized how much she missed her homeland; scathing editorials by two students on issues affecting our local professional football team; a "mass murderer" project by two students who were affected by reading *Helter Skelter*; more poetry in one month than my students had written in the previous 5 years altogether; a moving short story by a student who combined ideas from reading *The Outsiders* and my reading to them of "On the Sidewalk Bleeding": a humorous story about a young man who ends up on Skid Row because of those infernal *Time* magazine inserts that keep falling out while you try to read the magazine; two students (one from Special Ed., the other one of the top students) who without realizing it were both interested in the Vietnam war now collaborating on a project; letters to the principal and local police officials about an issue that directly affects many of the students; an interview with the two directors of a local church drop-in centre that is taking the community by storm, etc., etc.

I guess the final clincher has been the last two weeks of class. Two separate incidents have greatly affected my students. The first involved a local boy, an ex-student who was killed while trying to outrace a train at a crossing. He was very drunk and tried to run across the tracks before the train got there. The second was the Ben Johnson steroid incident, an item of discussion everywhere— in the staffroom and the classroom. I realize that in the past there was no other way I could have accommodated these events in my classroom, other than by responding to students' journal writing. Now I not only have the freedom to let them respond to these two events, but I have even been able to structure my "Mini-lessons" on what happened in the press (e.g., looking at "points of view" in writing). These are real and meaningful to my kids, and I have been able to allow them a chance to respond in an honest way (and teach them something at the same time). While I pray that we can use more pleasant events in the classroom, I realize now that the classes that were covering the friendly letter for the past two weeks really missed the boat.

Syd Korsunsky's passion about writing and reading, combined with an approach to teaching that allows students to be passionate about writing and reading, tells his kids that literacy is for making decisions, not for filling up writing folders.

He and the other teachers whose workshops are working are not looking for teacher-proof methods. They are looking for immersion in writing and reading. They avoid The Bogus Tradition and all the latest writing process gimmicks—special folders, notebooks, and webs—because they recognize that idiosyncrasy and diversity are the wellsprings of excellence. They are the teachers least likely to start a sentence with "My students love . . ." or "My students can't . . ." or "When my students write, they all . . . " because their own unpredictable experiences with literacy have compelled them to see and respond to individuals. They understand all of the ways that they use reading and writing in their own lives, and they work to create both open-ended possibilities for every student in the workshop *and* new standards of excellence. It is a heady combination.

Linda Rief (1989) recently observed:

> All teachers should be readers and writers, but teachers of language arts must be writers and readers. How many schools hire home economics teachers who do not cook or sew, industrial arts teachers who will not use power tools, coaches who have never played the game, art teachers who do not draw, Spanish teachers who cannot speak Spanish? Yet, how many prospective English teachers are asked in their interviews, "What are you reading? What are you writing?" (15)

When writing workshop works, teachers don't regard their own literacy as an extra, as enrichment. They may well have started out using *In the Middle* as a cookbook by borrowing the security of its structures to help them as they made radical changes in their methods. But they took the next, crucial step. They revealed themselves as readers and writers to their students and became the joyful mentors that kids will want to learn from, learn with, and emulate in the writing workshop.

7 ⫸ BRINGING IT ALL BACK HOME

"**B**UT DON'T YOU MISS THE KIDS?"

I resigned my job at Boothbay Region Elementary School after my daughter was born. I had taught junior high English for twelve years. Toward the end I worked harder than I ever have at anything to become a careful observer of my eighth graders. I watched them and listened to them, laughed with them and cried too, dreamed about them, wrote about them, and traveled everywhere sharing their accomplishments as writers and readers with other teachers. I was obsessed, and I was unbelievably happy. I learned a lot from those kids.

Since Anne's birth teachers have wondered, "But don't you miss the kids?" The answer is no. Except for twinges of my usual, irrational nostalgia for the group that left me the last June I taught, I do not miss eighth graders. And I'm as surprised as anyone by my response.

From the start Anne turned our lives upside down in all the ways that children humble their parents. During the first year she consumed our days and nights so thoroughly there wasn't a spare moment to reminisce about teaching—or to read anything, write anything, or tie my shoes. Then fairly soon, when the good stuff started happening, I became an observer again, this time of Anne. She is my classroom. If I'm seldom nostalgic for eighth graders, I am grateful to them for all the ways they prepared me to be a certain kind of parent to my daughter. Because I learned to learn from them, I can learn from Anne too. Although the connections between adolescents and a preschooler may seem tenuous at best, every day that Anne and I are together I see ways that my literate behavior at home is shaped by my experience as an eighth-grade English teacher.

Current literacy theory (Wells 1986; Newman 1985; Goelman et al. 1984) asks educators to learn from parents by extending the conditions of literate households into the primary classroom and beyond. I'd like to reverse the process and consider how my experience in a classroom organized as a workshop for readers and writers has affected my behavior with my daughter, now four years old. I am finding that the roots of my interactions with Anne run deep. More important, I am learning that children of every age can benefit from literate relationships with adults and that it is never too early or too late to begin a literary apprenticeship, at school or at home.

One summer morning my neighbor kneeled before Anne, age seventeen months, and laughed. The words came out rapid fire. "God, Nancie, doesn't she look like her daddy. Hello, little Anne. How are you? Fine? Are you going somewhere with your mommy? Are you going to the store? And who is this? Is this your doggy? Yes, it is. Do you love her? Yes you do." Sheila chatted, Anne beamed up at her, and I strangled an impulse to reach over and put my hand on Sheila's mouth. I recognized the same frustration I had felt when a new guidance counselor, meeting with my students for the first time, had answered every question she asked them. ("What are your hobbies? Swimming? Music? Skateboarding? Videos? What are your goals? High school? College? A job?") There seemed to be little understanding that patience through an awkward silence might lead to rewards on both sides.

I picked up the silent Anne and jiggled her while Sheila and I gossiped about doings in our neighborhood, then carried her back inside, set her in her little chair, and pulled up my big one. I wanted to listen to us.

NANCIE: Hi, Anne.

ANNE: . . . Hi.

N: How are you today?

A: . . . Good.

N: Where are Anne and Mum going?

A: . . . Store.

N: In the . . .

A: Car!

N: Yes, in Mum's car. Who did Anne just see?

A: . . . Shhhhh.

N: That's right. We saw Sheila and she gave you a cuddle. Does Anne love Sheila?

A: . . . Umhmm.

N: Okay. Are you ready, goose?

A: . . . Purse! Annie's purse!

N: Okay, okay, here it is. Hold my hand. C'mon, let's go.

A: . . . C'mon, let's go.

Some of our pauses lasted a full ten seconds. I made spaces for Anne and expected that she would fill them. She did. This talk wasn't novel, of course. Elements of our conversation had been repeated in dozens of other contexts, and Anne could probably predict both the questions I would ask and the spaces I would make. But long before this, elements of our conversation had also been repeated in thousands of writing conferences with eighth graders.

I think that much of my talk with Anne draws on my behavior in writing conferences. I spent a long time learning to slow down my approach to young writers—to initiate conferences with the predictable entrée "How's it coming?" (Calkins 1983) and then to wait sympathetically, sometimes through an awkward silence, for students to tell me how their writing was coming. I waited so they might make their own judgments about what was working and what needed more work, become conscious of their writing strategies through articulating them, and take big risks as writers. I waited in order to give them time to think. I wait for Anne so she can think, too.

Waiting did not come naturally to me as a teacher. I wonder if it would have as a parent, if I hadn't had the benefit of all those conferences. Children do learn from our talk, but I'm convinced that they learn at least as much from their own responses. Graves (1983) has pointed out similarities between the temporary structures or "scaffolds" (Bruner 1983) a parent uses to respond to a child's language and activity and the structures that teachers use in writing conferences. I know the parallels from the other side, as a teacher who learned to be still and listen and then became a mother. We adults, parents and educators, give children a gift when we make spaces for their talk, expect that children will fill them, and then build on the child's responses.

We can give the same gifts of time and patience to readers of all ages. The last year I taught, my students read an average of thirty-five books—fiction of all kinds, poetry, history, and biography. Their reading scores averaged at the 72nd percentile in a district where the 50th percentile was the norm. I think that their accomplishments were due to one factor. They read a lot. I ensured it by shelving the class sets of anthologies and the worksheets and purchasing a classroom library of good adolescent literature. Then I set aside three hours of class time each week for students to do nothing but read, allowed them to choose their own books, and talked with them about what they were reading or might read next. Time, responsibility for choice, and response were the foundations of the reading program; they are also the foundations of Anne's experience with books at home.

From the start we surrounded Anne with books. A surprise baby shower at an NCTE convention launched her library. Guests brought their favorite children's literature as gifts, and before Anne was born she owned fifty books. We have continued to buy and borrow many more. Anne needs books in her house for the same reason that eighth graders needed books in their classroom. The environment requires literature if it is to become literate. I wonder what we demonstrate about reading when we don't value books enough to make sure there is a good supply available, or when the only books in a classroom are basals and anthologies.

I also wonder what we show kids about reading when we won't trust them enough to choose their own books. Force-feeding a steady diet of my tastes in literature does no one good, adolescent or toddler. When I saw students' genuine involvement in the books that they selected for themselves, I stopped assigning books, even my favorites. It was hard to let go of the books I loved but necessary if eighth graders were to find the books that they loved. At home I stopped assigning books to Anne as soon as she was old enough to indicate her tastes— when, bolder than an eighth grader, she could snatch the book she wanted or smack the one she didn't. When she was sixteen months old, our read-aloud sessions began with me holding up her books one at a time. She would shake her head at each and say, "No, no, no, no," until I found the right one. "Yes! Moon! Moon!" she crowed when I finally showed her *Goodnight Moon* (Brown 1947).

As with eighth graders, I learned to accept that Anne's tastes in literature are not always mine. At nine months she already had favorites. She loved *Ten, Nine, Eight* (Bang 1983), *Corduroy* (Freeman 1968), *When Will It Snow?* (Hoff 1971), the *Alfie* books by Shirley Hughes, and *Brown Bear, Brown Bear, What Do You See?* (Martin 1967). She kissed the children's faces at the end of *Brown Bear* so often that the pages are forever stiff with dried spit. But she did not like books by Robert McCloskey, Minarik's *Little Bear* series, or *Madeline* (Bemelmans 1939)—all of which became favorites the following summer. Eighth graders had taught me that if I were patient and responsive their tastes would grow beyond Jim Kjelgaard and Judy Blume, so I know that Anne will grow through perhaps hundreds of phases in her life as a reader. I'll surround her with books that I think she will like, as I did my eighth graders, then respond to her choices and encourage new ones. I'll also look for books by Anne's favorite authors— currently Beverly Cleary, Shirley Hughes, and Mem Fox—just as I watched for new novels by Susan Beth Pfeffer, Robert Lipsyte, and Walter Dean Myers for my students. I'll take Anne to book- stores and let her graze just as I carted eighth graders to Book- land. And I'll remember with caution the basals and kits I ban- ished from my classroom and continue to offer Anne only whole pieces of the real thing, to be read aloud to her as many times as she chooses.

All of my eighth graders had reread at least one book, and some were devoted rereaders. S. E. Hinton's *The Outsiders* (1967) had a fanatical following of boys and girls who gave it multiple rereadings through junior high. I am a longtime re- reader of novels, from the dozen times I lived with *Little Women* to my traditional summer's breeze through Mary McCarthy's *A Charmed Life* (1954). And yet for years I forbade students to choose books they had already read. Somehow, when they reread it was cheating. Finally I came to understand Frank Smith's one rule for making learning to read easy: "Respond to what the child is trying to do" (1983, 24).

When eighth graders chose to reread, I began to respond to their reasons for rereading. They wanted the sense of security they derived from familiar characters in familiar situations and wanted to be with these friends once more. They wanted to notice how the author had written, something readers seldom do their first time through a good story. They wanted their emotions touched, to cry again or feel happy or scared again. They wanted to relax for a few days. Or they didn't know what else to read that they might like. My job was to understand the reader's response and offer help if I thought the reader needed it. Most often, students who reread did not need my help. They were helping themselves by returning to ground they had already covered. Rereading provided an important opportunity to practice fluent reading, to pick up speed through familiar territory and get better at what good readers do.

When Anne asks for the same books again and again, she, too, is learning what reading is all about. As she sits on my lap through multiple readings she develops a sense of story (Applebee 1978) that helps her anticipate such story features as "once upon a time," "happily ever after," and "the end." She uses illustrations as clues to what will happen in the story. She notices letters and words. She anticipates rhymes and rhythms, words, phrases, and sentences—she cannot wait to bellow "I'll call in the army!" along with General Pinch in *The Araboolies of Liberty Street* (Swope 1989) or furnish the right end rhymes to *Paddy Pig's Poems* (Charles 1989). Each time we reread a book, elements of Anne's response are different—new questions, new things she notices, new places where she can chime in to say the story with us. And each time certain elements remain—questions or comments she has repeated during many rereadings of a text, reading rituals she has created to complement the reading rituals that her father and I have introduced.

Every evening one of us invites Anne up on the sofa for stories, and many evenings in a row she brings the same books. For a whole month she wanted *Mufaro's Beautiful Daughters* (Steptoe 1987) and a version of *Snow White* that takes half an hour to read aloud. Whenever I was tempted to hide *Snow White*, I reminded myself that the payoff from this investment of time was already enormous. By the time she was two, Anne had started to retell her stories. Some days she sat on the sofa by herself, turning the pages and reciting her versions of *The Carrot Seed* (Krauss 1945), *The Tiger Who Came to Tea* (Kerr 1968), *When We Went to the Park* (Hughes 1985), and *Outside over There*

(Sendak 1981) among others. The stronger the rhythm or pattern of a book, the more likely that Anne would try to retell it. The following is her rendition, at twenty-five months, of the poem that forms the book *Here Are My Hands*. The text appears on the right; Anne's version, in italics, is on the left.

Here Are My Hands	Here Are My Hands
Here Are My Hands	Here Are My Hands
Bill Martin, Jr.	By Bill Martin, Jr. and
	John Archambault
	Illustrated by Ted Rand
Here are my hands for	Here are my hands for
catching and throwing.	catching and throwing.
Stopping and going.	Here are my feet for stop-
	ping and going.
My head for thinking and	Here is my head for
knowing.	thinking and knowing.
Here my nose for smelling	Here is my nose for
and blowing.	smelling and blowing.
Seeing and crying.	Here are my eyes for see-
	ing and crying.
Here are my ears for wash-	Here are my ears for wash-
ing and drying.	ing and drying.
Knees for falling down.	Here are my knees for
	falling down.
Here my neck for turning	Here is my neck for turn-
around.	ing around.
Here my cheeks for blush-	Here are my cheeks for
ing.	kissing and blushing.
Here are my teeth for	Here are my teeth for
chewing and brushing.	chewing and brushing.
Here my neck and my	Here is my elbow, my
elbow and chin.	arm, and my chin.
And here is my skin that	And here is my skin that
bundles me in.	bundles me in.
The end.	

Anne would occasionally touch the words when she retold a story, but her eyes were usually glued to the illustrations, from which she took her cues as a reader. Ted Rand's illustrations for *Here Are My Hands* are bold, lively, double-page spreads of a boy or girl in action. The appealing pictures and the rhyming text made retelling a natural, even irresistible, impulse when Anne picked up the book on her own. But the groundwork was laid over all the evenings that Anne and I cuddled on the sofa, saying the words and talking about the pictures together.

Anne started to behave like a reader because we learned to make reading easy. She doesn't need or want a new book every day. She loves new books, but she also needs and wants familiar structures and illustrations, rituals, and the security of buddies like Shirley Hughes's Alfie and Vera Williams's Rosa, just as my eighth graders wanted to go inside Ponyboy's mind again or take off on another adventure with The Three Investigators, Nancy Drew, or Dicey.

Eighth graders' wide reading had many tangible benefits. In addition to the rise in test scores, they reported reading more at home and buying more books of their own. For me, the most significant effect of their reading was on their writing. I noticed more and more occasions when elements from the literature they were reading showed up in the literature they were writing. The conclusion of Jennifer's short story was subtle and ambiguous— "like Susan Beth Pfeffer's writing," she explained. Tom's social studies report carried Frost's poem "Immigrants" as its epigraph because Laura had used a Frost poem similarly in a prizewinning essay the previous year. Sandy's story about a girl's first date was written first-person in extremely short paragraphs, in the same style as the novels by Bruce and Carol Hart that she had just finished reading.

As writers, students "borrowed" (Blackburn 1984) genres, themes, topics, and techniques. They borrowed from my writing and each other's, and from professional authors. The diversity of literature to which they were exposed in their reading class exerted a pervasive influence on their writing. In previous years, when the reading program consisted of anthologies, reading had exerted no discernible influence. Programmed instruction did not inspire eighth-grade authors. But once they started reading often and widely, I couldn't keep track of the effects that they and I saw everywhere. And, of course, the significant difference is that their writing improved. Reading taught them to be better writers.

The notebooks that I filled with the evidence of eighth graders' literary borrowings were the forerunners of a journal that

I started to keep at home when Anne was nineteen months old. These are a few early excerpts.

> 8/31/87
> Nancie: When will Daddy be home?
> Anne: Soon. Soon. NOW.
> (Syd Hoff's *When Will It Snow?*)

> 9/6/87
> When I put her lunch in front of her (chicken salad) she asked, "Hiawatha's chickens?" (Longfellow, Susan Jeffers's version)

> 10/5/87
> In our bedroom this afternoon she picked up a wire coat hanger, held it to her lips, and said, "Ida played her wonder horn to rock the baby still but never watched." (Sendak's *Outside over There*, the line exactly.)

> 10/22/87
> When Toby was paying our bill at Sarah's Pizza tonight, she stood under the neon Miller Lite sign in the window, looked out into the night, and announced, "The lights shine out into the street. Merry Christmas, Lucy and Tom! Merry Christmas, everyone!" (Final lines in *Lucy and Tom's Christmas*. L. and T. are looking out the window of their house with their Christmas tree lit up behind them.)

Because my students had left me so attuned to connections between reading and writing, I attended to the connections that Anne began to make between books and life almost as soon as she started to talk. Again, the influence of literature is everywhere. Anne is a different child—thinks differently, talks differently, and is starting to write differently—because of her exposure to the language, ideas, and features of children's literature. I began to categorize the ways that Anne is affected by the books we read to her, how she borrows from authors just as my eighth graders did, and from illustrators too.

The most obvious influence of literature is on Anne's oral language. Toddlers are sponges, and she was no exception. I expunged the phrase "No way" from my vocabulary after Anne used it to answer every question that I put to her during one very long afternoon. She picked up more interesting language from her books. When two-year-old Anne walked the length of our upstairs hall she chanted, "Heigh ho, heigh ho, it's home from work we go." If she wanted to hug our (justifiably) nervous dog, she commanded, like Max in Sendak's *Where the Wild Things Are,* "BE STILL." She ran through the house with her bookbag over her shoulder yelling, "My satchel is flying!" a variation on a line from *Dogger* (Hughes 1977). And because Sophie and her parents dine at a café in *The Tiger Who Came to Tea,* Anne campaigned every Saturday for lunch at the "Burger King Café."

Like every two-year-old, Anne attempted to regulate her parents' behavior, and sometimes her argument was literary, rather than the usual exercise in sheer willfulness. Shirley Hughes, who writes extensively about domestic situations, became Anne's favorite source for persuasive tactics. When she wanted me to fetch the bathrobe she got for Christmas she wheedled, "I want my robe like in *Lucy and Tom's Day.*" When I told her to come away from the banister around our upstairs landing she explained, "But I'm waiting at the gate for my mother and father," a line from *Lucy and Tom's 1.2.3.* And one morning, desperate to get me to sit down at her table and paint with her, she said, "Mama, come. Let's make Christmas cards with pictures of robins on them," as the children do in *Lucy and Tom's Christmas.*

Anne's background with books also shows up in her imaginative play, as the antics of the characters in stories and poems enrich her pretending. At Christmas she scrambled onto the kitchen table, stood up, and proclaimed, "To top of the porch, to top of the wall, now dash away, dash away ALL." On another winter's morning while Toby was showering, she took off her shoes and socks, rolled up her trousers, and pounded on the bathroom door. "What are you doing?" I asked. She replied, "I want my father to come out. I want to go and dig clams with my father," like Sal in *One Morning in Maine* (McCloskey 1952). Her shoes and socks also came off when she acted out *Alfie's Feet* (Hughes 1982). She plopped herself down by a hot air register, rested her feet on the edge, and explained, "I'm warming my toes by the fire." At twenty-six months Anne pretended the party in Minarik's *Little Bear's Friend* around the same register. "I'm

Emily. My Barbie will be Lucy. She's going to fall down. Mama, you're Little Bear. You will fix Lucy." I asked, "Who's Dad?" "He can be Owl," she responded. Then she asked her father for his pen so Emily could give it to Little Bear as a going-away present. On a half-dozen occasions she either dictated to me or scribbled the letter that Little Bear writes to Emily at the end of the book. At age four her favorite bathtub game is to don my shower cap, draw the shower curtain, and peek out, posed to recreate an illustration from *I Go with My Family to Grandma's* (Levinson 1986).

Anne's books also inspired object play, which Vygotsky characterizes as one precursor of writing (1978). One day when we were coloring she held up a brown marker and announced, "This is the house that Jack built." Another marker was the rat that ate the malt and so on, down to the farmer sowing his corn. At the post office a few days later a neighbor gave her a mailing tube to play with; Anne straddled it and recited "Ride a Cock Horse to Banbury Cross."

A fourth kind of knowledge that comes to Anne from books is a knowledge of books themselves. She remembers language, functions of text, and book features from one reading to the next and makes connections within and between texts. Because we usually tell the author's and illustrator's names when we read to her, she knows authors and illustrators. It was Anne who pointed out to us that Diane Goode had illustrated both *The Story of the Nutcracker Ballet* (Hautzig 1986) and *Watch the Stars Come Out* (Levinson 1985). When I read her a new book, Jeanne Titherington's *Big World, Small World* (1985), Anne said, "She wrote *A Place for Ben.*" At age two she added "The end" to most read-alouds, whether the words appeared or not, but she also understood that print represents language. She would point to a chunk of text and ask, "What does it say here? Read those words," most often in connection with an illustration that interested her. She also remembered information about authors ("Mama, is this a picture of Marc Brown and his two boys?"), could read the signatures in the few autographed books we own, and had an ever-increasing vocabulary for book features. She called down to me from her room one day, where she was pillaging a bookcase, "I found the dust jacket for *Miss Rumphius!*" (Cooney 1982). The first work of nonfiction to achieve favorite book status was Aliki's *How a Book Is Made* (1986), a fourth birthday present.

Finally, because Anne reads she has a knowledge of the world she could never gain from firsthand experience. As Gordon Wells (1986) has written:

> [T]hrough stories, children vicariously extend the range of their experience far beyond the limits of their immediate surroundings. In the process, they develop a much richer mental model of the world and a vocabulary with which to talk about it (152).

Anne's immediate surroundings are an island community off the Maine coast, but her books introduce her to people, places, concepts, and cultures far beyond her little world. There is not a year-round traffic light on our peninsula or island, but when we crossed the street Anne would inform me, "The red light says stop, and the green light says go" (*Bathwater's Hot* by Shirley Hughes). She has never eaten in a Chinese restaurant, but Mercer Mayer's critters do in *Just Grandpa and Me* (1985); Anne pilfered two cinnamon sticks from my spice cabinet and explained, "These are my chopsticks." No one we know plays the accordian, but Anne rolled her Fisher Price piano on its side, heaved it up, clasped it against her chest, and staggered around the house saying, "Look at my 'ccordian. I'm playing the 'ccordian like Rosa," in *Something Special for Me* by Vera B. Williams (1983). From *Alfie's Feet* by Shirley Hughes (1982) she taught herself left from right and how to put on her own boots.

One sunny morning Anne climbed aboard the foot I was swinging and asked for a ride. "Come on," she said. "We're going on a boat to America. Far across the water." She didn't have the word yet, but thanks to *Watch the Stars Come Out* (Levinson 1985) she already knew a bit about emigration. And as Wells's research suggests, I believe that the "mental model of the world" afforded Anne through listening to stories will serve her well in every area of the curriculum when it comes time for her to go to school.

I mentioned that I write down Anne's literary allusions in a special notebook (Figure 7–1), one of three written records. Another is her baby book, in which I note milestones under the headings provided in the book. The third is a bound book for recording anecdotes about things she does, says, and knows (Figure 7–2). This may seem like a crazy amount of record keeping,

◄ FIGURE 7–1 ►

Excerpt from a Record of Anne's Literary Allusions

Sunday 14
Made me sit down with her at her desk, to color with colored pencils. "Let's make some Christmas cards." (Like T & L in *Lucy & Tom's Christmas*.)
Put a ribbon across her face, from ear to ear. "I'm an Indian. Like Hiawatha."
ST. VALENTINE'S DAY

Monday 15
Took off her shoes & socks in the diningroom, sat down by the register & rested her feet on the edge. "I'm warming my toes by the fire." (*Alfie's Feet*) Then put Barbie by the fireplace "to warm her toes."
Pretended a parade in Reny's Dept. Store. Marched down the long central aisle reciting "A parade! A parade! A rum a tee tum! I know a parade by the sound of the drum!" (Catherine Snow's poem "Parade.")
WASHINGTON'S BIRTHDAY OBSERVED

Tuesday 16
Called me "Tiger" all morning, after another tea party where we took turns pretending to be Sophie and the *Tiger Who Came to Tea* (a game she initiates daily).
Came downstairs in the black patent leather shoes from Bloomingdale's. "Here I am. I'm Eloise!"

Wednesday 17
ASH WEDNESDAY

Thursday 18
She asks: "Who has a soft brown stuffed dog?" I reply, "Dogger." "No, not Dogger." "I don't know. Who?" She runs to her room & gets the dog that Alfred gave her for Christmas. "You be Kristen and I'll be Jamaica. Look! Look! Here's your dog!" (*Jamaica's Find*).
She picked up my old copy of *How to Get Pregnant*, pointed to the photo of the bald, bearded author on the back, and said, "That's a picture of me when I was two months old."

Friday 19
Riding her hobbyhorse, recited, "Ride a cock horse to Banbury Cross."

Saturday 20
Pretended a party on the register in the dining room. "I'm Emily. Barbie is Lucy. She's going to fall down. You're Little Bear. (to me) You'll fix Lucy." I asked, "Who's Dad?" "He's Owl." Asked Toby for his pen so "Emily" could give it to "Little Bear" as a going-away present. (*A Friend for Little Bear*)
"I'm crawling backward like Annie Rose." (*Alfie's Feet*)

FIGURE 7-2

Excerpt from an Anecdotal Journal

5/30 cont'd

At dinner last night Toby asked Anne, "What's that on your face?" She replied, "A booger."

Her favorite doll of the week is Chuck, a little Cabbage Patch Kid with bendable legs. "Sit, Chuck!" she instructs him. She still loves Alexander very much and calls her "Akka".

Now that the days are sunny and warm Anne wants to be outside. She takes my hand & drags me to the kitchen door: "Mum, mum, mum, outside, outside, outside."

She also drags me to the refrigerator and points. We keep her pad of paper & colored pencils on top. She'll sit at her little table & draw until she has used every color. The whole time she moans, "Aaaa, Aaaa, Aaaa" as if she were writing her name.

Q&A

What's your name?   Aaahhh.
Where do you live?   May
How old are you?   Sicksa
What's your daddy's name?   Toe
Where does Nana live?   Newwarka

5/31/87

Anne asked for the Peter Rabbit Pop-Up Book by name. She recognized it in her bookshelf by its spine ("Petey, mum, Petey"), and took my hand & put it on the book.

Tonight she was inconsolable: "Jraw, Jraw, jraw!" We finally decoded. She wanted to draw.

6/1/87

We went through all of her books, one at a time. I'd pick one up and she'd shake her head and say, "No." No, no, no until "Moon! Moon!" She's reading Good-night but I can't help it. My experience as a teacher who observed her students—as a teacher-researcher—has changed me forever. Everywhere I look I see data.

For years I studied the writing and then the reading of eighth graders. I wrote down the things they said and did, read their writing over many months with an eye to patterns in their growth, and interviewed them often about their uses and views of written language. I made sense of my observations, asking "What does this mean for my teaching?" And I described my students, their work, and the things I had learned in articles and a book. Research and teaching went hand in hand, and data arose naturally in this interactive community where a group of kids and I spent our days interpreting, analyzing, informing, criticizing, collaborating, inventing, and questioning. As I filled notebooks, my teaching became more patient and more sensible. More importantly, my classroom research taught me to focus on what eighth graders *could do* as writers and readers, instead of falling back into a deficit-model perspective.

The day that Anne was born her father joked, "Please, no case studies." I laughed and agreed, but I didn't realize then how ingrained the data-gathering habit was. As soon as we arrived home from the hospital I started writing and saving: pieces of hair, photographs, and baby souvenirs, but also every scrap of paper on which Anne has made her mark. This data serves me as a mother, just as classroom research helped my teaching. In the midst of the dailiness of teaching or parenting it is easy to lose track of a child's slow growth, and harder still sometimes to notice and respond to what a child is trying to do.

At eighteen months, Anne was paging through a big book version of *Yes Ma'am* (Melser and Cowley 1980). She pointed to the word "How" and said "H." I couldn't think where she had learned the letter, until I went back to my journal and found an entry describing how she had traced the letters on my Harvard T-shirt and asked me to say them. I knew that environmental print played a role in children's literary awareness, but I assumed that Anne was too young to notice. I learned it was time to start mentioning more of the words that appear in Anne's environment. She has a little grocery cart filled with miniature cans and boxes. Toby read her the writing on each container when they pretended to shop, and Anne read many of the labels to me the next day when it was my turn to be the clerk.

Another day I made a note about all of the words that Anne could recognize. At twenty-one months she could identify her own name, plus Mom, Dad, Books (our dog), Grammy, Nana, and the names of her cousins, words that had two things in common. They were names of people she loved, words she would want to know, and each began with an uppercase letter. I wrote all ten words on a piece of paper, asked Anne to read them to me, and listened. She read, "M for Mom, D for Dad, B for Books," and so on. Anne used the initial, uppercase letter as a clue for identifying the word. This was a clue for me to recognize that Anne might be ready to talk about the alphabet. And because I had learned a hundred times over, from my students and Anne, that children learn best in whole contexts, we covered the refrigerator with a magnetized alphabet so she could touch and move all of the letters together and see their similarities and differences. At twenty-six months, through casual conversations and play, Anne identified every letter. She did not identify letters, however, when they appeared in isolation on "Sesame Street," and I was interested in thinking about why.

The ways that children benefit when an adult finds them interesting are obvious. The attention and collaboration that result help move learning forward in important ways. But careful observation and reflection serve the adult, too. Classroom research kept my teaching interesting and fresh; it is the best antidote I know to teacher burnout. The observations I make of Anne's behavior have the same effect. I love her to pieces because she is my daughter, but I love being Anne's mother because the personal satisfaction is so intense. She captured my heart and my mind. And once she started to write, the experience just got richer.

I remember the day I set up a center for writing materials in my classroom. I had spent my entire budget for language arts at stationery stores in Portland, and the array covered one counter: all kinds of paper and markers, stationery and envelopes, postcards, calligraphy pens, white-out fluid, lined ditto masters, markers, rulers, staplers, fasteners, book-binding materials. My students' excitement was palpable. They had been writing on yellow paper, the kind with chunks of wood still floating in it, for so long that a range of decent materials for writing was an unimagined luxury.

It is easy for teachers to underestimate the importance of tools for writing unless we write ourselves. Once I started, I wanted thick pads of narrow-lined paper and black, fine-point markers. I also needed scissors and tape, white-out, a stapler, paper clips, scrap paper, and file folders. The physical act of writing—of noting, drafting, revising, editing, proofreading, and saving—required a writer's tools. So I made certain that my students, too, had the materials they needed in order to do what authors do.

A range of materials for writing had another effect on my students. Different kinds of utensils and papers suggested new formats and genres for their writing. Stationery inspired correspondence, calligraphy pens inspired illuminated greeting cards and poetry posters, lined ditto masters inspired memos to the other kids in the class, book-binding materials inspired individual volumes of poetry, advice, or stories for younger children. The opportunity to choose not only topic but also medium was crucial to eighth graders' discoveries of what writing is good for.

By the time she was two Anne already had a taste of what writing is good for, and I think her sense of writing, too, had something to do with materials. I took another page from the experience of my students and provided Anne with plenty of ways to make her mark and plenty of places to make it. The best investment we made, apart from books, was a set of artist's pencils—thirty colors, water soluble, soft lead. They gave her more pleasure than any crayons or markers. At sixteen months she would holler "Jraw! Jraw! Jraw!" until one of us translated and fetched her pencils. She liked to sit at her little table with her own pad of white paper, thick enough so it would anchor itself, and jraw for half an hour or more.

At age two Anne liked markers (once she could uncap them by herself), water-colors, stamps and inkpads, stickers, post-it notes, Play-Doh, her magic slate and little blackboard, and my pens. We sat together at the kitchen table catching up on our correspondence; Anne's consisted of cards that she made from wallpaper samples and decorated with drawings and stickers. She sent these to her grandparents and cousins and anticipated each day's trip to the post office in hopes that our box would hold mail addressed to her. She also wrote shopping lists and dictated or scribbled innumerable letters to Santa, each one the same: "Dear

Santa, Bring Anne a candy cane and an umbrella" (the last year that Santa got off so easy).

It is tempting to view Anne's early scribbles as merely charming, but I think they were much more than that. Anne knew that written language carries meaning, that writing is a way to communicate with people far away and to remember things. Over the past two years the scribbles became strings of random letters, then words, then phrases and sentences. Anne is a serious inventive speller. Her writing repertoire includes signs (KEP OT and NO MOMS NO DADS), letters to friends (DR MAYA U R MI BST FRND I LOVE U), and captions on drawings (KDLBR for cuddlebear and CNDRLA for Cinderella). In the blank books with construction-paper covers that we make at home, she draws her versions of *The Wizard of Oz, Snow White,* and *The Lion, the Witch and the Wardrobe* and labels each picture. And while I sit trying to invent a new speech, she is at my elbow inventing her own stories: "[It was] FBRRE [February] A L [little] GRL NAMD ANNE LEE WZ PAN [playing] DLS . . . " Because she sees her father and me writing, Anne thinks that writing is something that grown-ups do, and she wants in on it.

Gordon Wells found that children who were among the most accomplished writers by age nine or ten were much more likely to have parents who themselves wrote frequently, particularly lists, memos, and notes for themselves. I have made a point of writing with and around Anne for the same reasons that I sat down in my classroom and wrote with eighth graders. I hope to model how and why an adult uses written language, to show how writing changes my life. Among other reasons, I write to figure things out, to amuse myself and others, to inform, complain, remember, gossip, make a record, celebrate, thank, inquire, persuade, capture happy times, work through sad times, and make money. But long before I was a published author, eighth graders thought that I was a writer because I sat among them and wrote. These days I pull up a chair at Anne's little table, and together we figure out what we'll buy for dinner, tell her Grammy, or write in our little books.

There is an overriding reason for engaging in literate relationships with children, either at school or home. Of course such relationships are healthy, productive, and stimulating. They are also an incredible amount of fun. I was happy as a teacher because my students gave me so much to laugh and cheer about. Even their most awkward attempts as readers and writers were cause for celebration. Each time a writer risked a new technique or a reader a new genre, I saw growth. At some point every one of my students found the same satisfaction in writing and reading as I do because I expected they would love these things as I do.

This is the most important lesson that I carried home with me. Toby and I expect that Anne will love reading and writing. I've learned not to be afraid to nudge her in the direction of literacy, to help make it happen by giving her time, space, response, books, and materials for writing and drawing. I've learned not to wait to see if she is the kind of kid who likes writing and reading. I've learned that Anne's brain is built to have fun with language. I never yearn for school because I am so busy laughing and cheering at Anne's attempts and noting the genuine pleasure that she finds in literature and language.

One day I took Anne to the supermarket and over her usual, strenuous objections strapped her into a cart, then started wheeling her up and down the aisles. We were browsing at the deli counter when she looked up and saw her reflection in the strip of mirror that's angled over the cheeses. She admired herself for a moment, then burst into verse:

> Her lips blood red,
> her hair like night,
> her skin like snow,
> her name SNOW WHITE.

That is why I don't miss the kids.

8 AFTER
IN THE MIDDLE

NINETY PERCENT OF MY LETTERS FROM TEACHERS BEGIN "DEAR NANCIE."

Dear Nancie,

As I started to write to you, my immediate impulse was to call you by your first name because you reveal so much of yourself in your writing, I feel I know you. As I finish *In the Middle,* it just seems I'm reading an old friend. I hope you take this as a compliment. I also contemplated driving over to school to type this, but somehow I knew it wouldn't matter if I sat on my front porch and wrote you a first draft in longhand.

Dear Nancie,

When I read your book I felt you were sharing personal experiences in my living room over a good glass of wine, and I found myself talking back—out loud yet.

Dear Nancie,

Thanks, thanks, thanks, thanks, thanks for writing *In the Middle,* a book far more liberating to me than *The Feminine Mystique.* Yippee.

135

Before *In the Middle*, I thought that an author wrote a book, stuffed it into an envelope, mailed it off, and hoped for a few kind reviews. Instead *In the Middle* has taken on a life of its own, and its author, who I've come to think of as The Other Nancie Atwell, is living a life of her own with thousands of teacher friends from across the country. She is the voice it took me twelve drafts to get right, and she seems to have struck a chord.

It wasn't until the eighth draft of the first chapter that The Other Nancie Atwell emerged, when I settled on a first-person voice and a narrative format, in hopes that I might demonstrate what was possible for teachers and kids instead of dictating methods in the third person. *In the Middle* became the story of me and my students and our struggles to make sense of school, and I became the rueful, insightful, cheerful first-person that my husband sometimes wishes he were married to when he finishes reading a manuscript with my name on it. When I can do it well, writing gives me a voice that engenders a feeling of kinship with other teachers, and in writing *In the Middle* I tried to create a place where the truth could be spoken without embarrassment and sparks of recognition could ignite between a reader and me whenever our minds met on its pages. So I am delighted by the feelings of communion that my story has given rise to.

In the Middle may also have struck a chord because it attempts to present teaching as an intellectual process but in a practical way. By showing a teacher revising her teaching in light of her own and others' discoveries, the book has given other teachers permission to change—to view their teaching as a process, to abandon commercial materials and programs as a prism for thinking about language learning, and to focus on students, on what they know and need to know next and on the actual behaviors of writers and readers, as opposed to the joyless nonsense of *Warriner's* and dittoes. Their letters show me that *In the Middle* nudges teachers to discover how writing and reading can take on as much meaning for their students as they did for the eighth graders in a small school on the coast of Maine. As one teacher wrote, "I had to set a rule not to read the book at bedtime because it gets me so excited by the possibilities in what my students and I do."

The letters from readers have challenged, confirmed, and stretched my thinking about the teaching of English. They have deepened my respect for the lives of teachers and the extraordinary settings in which many teachers struggle to teach as they believe they should. And the letters have told me better than any review where *In the Middle* succeeded and where it failed.

Correspondence has come from junior and senior high schools in every corner of the country, from instructors of the gifted and talented and of English as a second language, from teachers in junior colleges, kindergartens, and elite private high schools, from undergraduates majoring in English education, special education and math teachers, even a professor of law. Their letters have taught me that the processes I wrote about are not unique to eighth graders. Although I observed writing, reading, and learning among junior high kids, writing, reading, and learning are human activities that cut across age, ability level, and ethnic background. In terms of their language learning, middle school kids are not a separate species. All of us, ages four to ninety-four, want our reading and writing to be meaningful, to make sense, and to be good for something. And teachers of all ages and subjects want to sponsor authentic contexts for learning and respond to their students as individuals, not as classes of quiz scores to be averaged or worksheets to be corrected.

In the Middle did not go unnoticed by companies that publish worksheets. I have received numerous invitations to create materials and texts based on the book, letters urging me to influence teachers in a positive direction by making things easier for them. I appreciate the interest, but my goal is not to make things easier for teachers. Our students need all the choices in the world, and they need teachers who know how to help kids discover their options. This is hard work, and there are no shortcuts to an individual teacher's understanding of language processes or individual students. But this is the hard work that makes teaching interesting. When we act as learners in our classrooms and take responsibility for our teaching, we invite surprises, satisfaction, and a new affinity with our students—things that we could never order from a catalogue. *In the Middle* has fostered my own knowledge by opening up a dialogue with others. Writing a textbook, telling others what to do in a monologue, could only close things down for me as a learner.

The remainder of my correspondence is from the students of teachers who have established their classrooms as places for reading and writing. Some kids write out of sheer joy in the newness of the workshop experience:

Dear Mrs. Atwell,

I love our new reading and writing program! In the beginning of the year I thought I'd hate it. When I got used to it, I loved it! Last year we were assigned things to write and read. This year is awesome because we can get anything we want to read or we can think of anything to write without getting told! Thank you very much! You made reading and writing come alive!

In reply I pointed out that he and his teacher were the ones who had made reading and writing come alive. *In the Middle* may have acted as a catalyst, but what is happening in that classroom belongs to the teacher and her students. The heartening truth is that a book can't change people's lives. People do that for themselves.

A Michigan fourth grader wondered:

Dear Nancie Atwell,

How do you find enough time to write? Whenever I'm out of school and I try to write it seem impossible. When I try to write I can only write for about a half an hour, and then I want to do something else.

I responded in part:

Once I started writing, I discovered that I had to make a time or I would never get down to it. If I wait until I am "inspired," I produce almost nothing. So I made a schedule and I stick to it. One thing that surprised me is how much better my writing is and how much more I enjoy it when I have a regular routine. I also pace myself and take short breaks, to get a drink of water or tickle my dog. Then I come back, read what I've written, play with it, and continue drafting. When the time is up, I'm ready to be with other humans again. And when the next day's writing time arrives, I'm itching to get back to my desk.

This is something that I didn't know about myself until I wrote it. I haven't always enjoyed writing. I used to dread it and did anything I could to get out of it. I was grateful for the opportunity to discover the truth in something that I had been telling kids for years: the satisfaction of writing comes over time as we finish pieces of writing that we like and come to trust that we can do so again.

Letters from kids have also stopped me in my tracks. Last spring two students wrote:

> Dear Ms. Atwell,
>
> We liked the idea of writing lab in the beginning, but now we're having constant writer's block. In fact it's getting to be quite boring. We do not feel we are creative enough to write the quality pieces required by this program. In your book you stated that the writing program would be a good program for all junior high students. Some people in our class can write and write and never run out of ideas. Their stories are always full of creation, but we do not feel we are able to keep up with the other kids in the class that are much more creative than we are. Our teacher just tells us to get to work. What do you suggest your students do?

In my response I had to level with the kids.

> On occasion, I did have students who feel as you do about writing, and I tried hard to be sensitive to and respond to "slumps" in their experiences as writers. In the workshop, it was my job—one of my jobs—to help kids through their writer's block and keep the writing fresh and vital. So I might do a series of mini-lessons— brief talks at the start of the workshop—on new kinds of writing to try. Or I might announce a new class magazine for my kids to contribute to, or share information about a writing contest. Or in mini-lessons I might show the class some new techniques that kids could try to improve their writing. I would definitely confer with blocked writers, interviewing them to help them find ideas that they cared about. And I would schedule group share sessions so that the whole class had opportunities to talk about, and try to solve, their writing problems.

If this response doesn't come too late in the school year to be of use to you, perhaps you might ask your teacher to schedule a group meeting so that you two could discuss your dilemma with her and the other kids and brainstorm solutions together.

I have had many letters from students about *In the Middle,* and hundreds of letters from teachers. Most are enthusiastic about writing because they've seen what it can do for them. I wish you all good luck as you try to discover what writing can do for you, what satisfaction it can bring.

Of course writing doesn't always bring satisfaction. It doesn't always bring anything. The more I write, observe writers, and read about writing, the more idiosyncrasy I have to allow for in students' literate behaviors. But the teacher's role in helping young writers is constant. This is not a laissez-faire approach. In the classrooms that are most successfully organized as workshops, the teacher:

- ► *expects* that every student will write, read, and find satisfaction in literacy
- ► organizes a predictable environment
- ► makes regular, sustained time in class for writing and reading
- ► allows choices from day one of topic, genre, pacing, and audience
- ► works with whole pieces of writing and whole pieces of literature, not paragraphs or excerpts or chapters
- ► offers response while individuals are engaged in the acts of writing and reading and moves among the students
- ► publishes students' writing and helps writers find real audiences
- ► helps readers find real audiences for their reading
- ► serves as an editor of final drafts
- ► teaches skills, conventions, and strategies to individuals in context
- ► keeps records of students' growth and helps students to keep their own records
- ► evaluates writing and reading for growth over time, in collaboration with students
- ► uses mini-lessons or some other forum as an opportunity to create a frame of reference for students to think together

about writing and reading, to create a group "lore" about
literacy
- ► reads literature for himself or herself and shares it
- ► writes literature for himself or herself and shares it
- ► and acts like a joyful reader and writer to whom students
  would wish to apprentice themselves.

Although I tried to convey the significance and complexity
of the workshop teacher's roles in *In the Middle,* my mail reminds
me, powerfully, that no way of teaching is teacher-proof. But it
also sends me back to the book, to a message that I hoped would
be implicit on every page. *In the Middle* is about how a teacher
found and solved her own problems. When I receive letters that
contain thirty questions about implementing workshops, invari-
ably the authors haven't acknowledged the problems of their
teaching situations, haven't presented themselves as writers and
readers who demonstrate literacy for students, haven't thought
enough about *why* they are teaching as they are teaching. The
result, all too often, is practices that contradict each other and
confuse and frustrate the kids.

I wonder what message is conveyed to students about the
teacher's seriousness of purpose when the workshop teacher
assigns exercises from a grammar textbook? When the teacher
dictates writing topics for the first half of the school year, or
forbids the writing of fiction, or tells students that they must
write X number of finished pieces and read X number of pages or
books representing X genres, or requires a dialogue journal entry
after every fifty pages read, or asks the same kinds of questions in
the dialogue journals that are written in the teacher's manual
of the anthology he or she abandoned, or gives mini-quizzes on
mini-lessons, or writes all over kids' papers in conferences, or
considers the publication of student writing a frill but still expects
perfect final copies? Kids understand that these are mixed mes-
sages. They rebel or withdraw or simply go through the motions,
and I receive a fat envelope of questions about coping with
"problem students." I don't have magical answers. Solutions to
teaching problems cannot be prescribed long distance by a
stranger. They grow from a teacher's examination of what he or
she is doing and why and from consultation with local experts,
namely one's colleagues and students.

Many of the questions that teachers ask in their letters have
raised pertinent issues about our roles in a workshop, and I am

learning through answering them—and finding the holes in *In the Middle*. Several teachers wrote, "How did you keep up with the dialogue journals?" I responded to the journals for up to an hour every afternoon before I went home. If the volume was heavy I kept my responses brief. Once my students got beyond plot synopses, usually by November, I was eager to see what they had written about their reading and couldn't wait to crack open the journals. I also wrote letters during the workshop—it was a workshop for me, too—as well as read my own books and made the rounds at the start of class to see what everyone else was reading.

Other teachers asked, "How did you ever read all the books your kids were reading?" No one has read every book or ever has to pretend to. I realized that I have conversations all the time about books I haven't read in which my friends teach me about the texts they have read, helping me decide whether I want to read them, too. We might best look at reading conferences and dialogue journals not just as vehicles for teaching our kids, but as forums for us to learn from them and then to help them decide what they will do next.

In answering the question, I also realized that I didn't learn about adolescent literature merely through reading it. I learned at least as much through the letters I wrote in students' dialogue journals. My best responses to students were the ones that taught me something I didn't know I knew. My worst responses are those in which I am going through the motions, and I cringe when I reread them. In hindsight I see myself asking questions to which I already know the answers ("Who are the main characters in *The Outsiders?*"), making dumb assumptions about what kids are or aren't doing ("You're not finishing books because you're lazy"), pretending to be interested in something I'm not ("Why, I'm a big fan of Louis L'Amour and Doctor Who just like you!"), and congratulating kids for having an opinion ("What a great letter. I'm so glad you shared your thoughts with me. They're really very interesting.")—which doesn't mean that I never congratulated kids on their letters. I often told them what fascinated me about their responses or what I learned from them. This is not the same as a patronizing pat on the back that ignores the ideas that the student has raised.

Looking back through the dialogue journals, I think that the most helpful responses echo the ways that I talk with my friends.

This is frank, opinionated, comfortable chat. And when I do ask questions, they're sparked by curiosity, not a sense of teacher obligation. When a teacher writes to me, "I put some of your kids' letters on transparencies to show my students what I had in mind, but I'm still getting superficial plot synopses," I respond, "Give it time, but also look at your own letters. Are they modeling the ways that you hope your students will engage with books?"

In our responses in reading conferences and dialogue journals, one good question is more than enough. If we really want to take kids inside books, that one good question will probably be some variation on the questions we ask our friends when we talk with them about books: How did you feel about the book? What made you feel this way? What did you think of the writing? Why do you think the author wrote it this way? When we help kids focus on issues of craft and their own responses—on how a book was written and how it affected them—we encourage an active, critical stance as readers. We *show them* how to come inside.

Along with questions on conferring about literature, teachers inquire about writing conferences. Neither seems to come easily. For most of us conferences about drafts in progress are such a radical departure from what we used to do that it takes a long time to get a sense of how they work, for us and for the kids. The most common questions about writing conferences have to do with their length:

Dear Nancie,

My greatest weakness is conferring. I recognize the need to confer with as many students as possible each class, but I am fortunate if I speak with six people during the thirty-five minutes following each mini-lesson. One problem lies with my students' uncertainty about their writing—many are unable to identify one or two elements in their drafts (other than, perhaps, the lead) to which they need response. . . . My "How's it going?" is met all too often with "Okay, I guess" although the student's eyes seem to suggest things are not as okay as he'd like. A second problem is the length of the pieces my students write. It is difficult to confer briefly on anything except the lead because their pieces are often several pages long.

Except for poems, brief letters, and memos, I seldom listened to whole pieces of writing. I learned to accept that there were pieces that I would not see until they came to me for editing. My role was not to hear every word that every student wrote, but to be available to help as many writers as possible during each class. A couple of summers ago, after I had taught a writing workshop for teachers, one of the participants wrote to me, "Now I see how you keep your conferences with kids so brief. You moved on and were gone before I realized you were finished. There's no closure: it's all 'middle.' Very businesslike."

I also used mini-lessons to teach students techniques to improve their writing—to troubleshoot their own pieces—and gradually, over time, they internalized the concepts and vocabularies of writers and brought these to their conferences with me and with each other. And I used mini-lessons to teach kids explicitly what to do in conferences: how to tell me about their pieces, strategies, and problems, how to read parts that are going well or parts they need help with, how to describe where they think they're going with the piece or how the writing surprised them. And in addition to asking "How's it going?" I learned from Linda Rief to ask, "How may I help you?"

I taught them that not only was it physically impossible for me to listen to every word they wrote, but that I didn't want to. If the writing teacher only listens to and analyzes whole pieces, writes advice or changes on papers, or sends pieces submitted for editing back to students for revisions in content, then he or she has taken responsibility for the writing and kids will look to the teacher to "fix" their writing all year long—and that teacher will burn out, fast.

My best advice about writing conferences is *wait*. We have to trust ourselves and the kids and remember that over a whole year of conferences, mini-lessons, and writing, our students will grow as writers and we will grow as responders and teachers.

The teachers who may have to wait longest for signs of student growth are those with whole classes of low-tracked readers or writers. When they write to ask for help in implementing workshops, I confess that this is the hardest work of all, not because of the nature of the kids but because of the administrative ignorance that puts such students in situations where they have few opportunities to collaborate with or learn from peers who are good at or like writing and reading. I was fortunate to be able to mainstream Boothbay's resource room students into my writing and reading workshops, and many of the written pieces and journal entries reproduced in *In the Middle* are the work of special education students. They succeeded in the workshop because they were surrounded by every kind of student, and because I finally learned to expect as much from them as I did the other kids.

At the beginning of the school year, classes of low-tracked students will have to take the teacher's word for it that literacy can be good for something. They will need a patient teacher who presents writing and reading as the best things on the face of the earth, who demonstrates his or her own passion as a writer and reader, who models every day what a good writer and reader does, and who believes that even the lowest-level kids will behave like writers and readers. I can't stress enough the importance of the teacher's expectations in convincing remedial students that they *will* write and they *will* read and that this year it's going to be the real thing.

In teaching reading, the books that low-level readers will respond to are the same titles listed in the back of *In the Middle*. These are the books that will both appeal to them and help them learn to read. I suggest that remedial teachers avoid high-interest-low-level materials and prescribed reading lists and, instead, read like crazy so that they can knowledgeably recommend Pfeffer, Duncan, Hinton, Blume, Roth, and Bennett. And they need to talk with their low-ability readers about their tastes and interests and then personally recommend great adolescent literature that they think each student will love, regardless of reading level. Every September at least a half a dozen students entered grade eight reading at the third- or fourth-grade level, and every year I talked with them as if they were readers and watched them grow toward fluency as they read the same loved titles as their more able friends. Time and choice are important, but for these kids the teacher's individual responses to them, their tastes, and their troubles will be another key.

As I listen to other teachers describe the circumstances of their teaching, I appreciate my mixed-ability groupings and schedule: two periods a day with each of my eighth-grade classes was a genuine luxury. But I most appreciate my good fortune to have found myself in a school system where for one brief shining moment, nobody was trying to force the adoption of a K–12 coordinated curriculum. That situation changed with the departure of several school board members and a superintendent who liked and trusted teachers and had allowed us to learn together. I realized then that an administration that didn't understand or share a commitment to literacy could actually subvert good teaching. And I recognized that teachers might have to negotiate for permission to improve their teaching—or even contemplate leaving a school system that requires them to teach badly in order to prepare students for more poor teaching.

On occasion a teacher will ask for advice about integrating mandated commercial materials in the workshop, from spelling, vocabulary, and grammar programs to kits and worksheets that mimic the format of the standardized tests used in their districts. Although I understand the politics of such situations, I won't pretend that these materials have anything to do with writing and reading. If an administration can't be persuaded to trust a teacher to develop his or her own systems for teaching conventions and vocabulary, methods that build on students' real experiences with literacy in the workshop, then the teacher might carve out a period in the day or week to zip through the required program—and respect students by not trying to convince them that these activities will improve their real writing and reading. In districts that require kids to submit to standardized tests, teachers can call a halt to the workshop and prep students for the test—its content and its format—by telling them exactly what to expect, giving them sample items, discussing how to read passages (how to determine what a test question is really after and eliminate unlikely answers), and teaching them how to write to a prompt in a timed setting.

The teachers who have been most successful in gaining acceptance for workshop methods are those who can articulate exactly what they are going to do, what students will do, and why: in short, teachers who have a theory of language learning. They are the individuals who can approach whoever is in charge and seek permission to pilot a workshop for a year or semester (or else decide that it's easier to ask forgiveness than permission and just close their doors and begin). At the end of the time they come back to their administration or department head with sample writing folders, lists of conventions that their students have learned, lists of the kinds of writing that showed up, lists of the concepts that the teacher introduced in mini-lessons, conferences, and dialogue journals. And they can say, "Compare this with *anybody's* scope and sequence. We need to consider whether we're cheating our students because our curriculum so limits what they do in our classrooms."

Other teachers have been successful in carving out blocks of time to institute writing workshops—three days a week for a whole school year, or five days a week for a semester, or every other quarter, or six weeks on and six weeks off—in order to give kids the experience of real writers and at the same time cover a syllabus. I have also learned of interesting variations on reading workshop within established curricula, modifications in which teachers worked hard to introduce elements of choice.

For example, teachers have used required basals or anthologies discriminately, asking their students to skim the book and select the pieces they wish to read. Then they have abandoned the teacher's manual in order to pose honest questions, assign reading logs, or try dialogue journals. And they've used the extra time they gained each week for independent reading and response.

Similarly, when the literature curriculum specifies a year's worth of titles, the teacher doesn't have to require that students read every word of every work. Students can be asked to sample the required texts in order to create opportunities for self-selected reading—that sometimes includes the formerly required texts.

If the curriculum requires the introduction of a particular genre, the teacher can provide multiple copies of different books representing the genre, then allow students to choose a book and group themselves based on their choices. In an elective course, the teacher might help each student select books that will fit the course title. Or the teacher can introduce a range of titles in mini-lessons and allow students to choose among them, then assign silent reading, dialogue journals, prompted or open-ended reading logs, small-group and large-group share sessions, and so on. All of these modifications involve a teacher treating kids like readers in the hope that students who become genuinely involved with books in school will have embarked on a lifetime's involvement with literature.

Finally, teachers who write to me wonder how to manage students who distract others and disrupt the workshop. Movement *is* a necessary feature of workshops. When students are engaged as readers and writers, they will need to return and sign out books, fetch their reading journals, write responses then deliver them to others for their responses, sharpen pencils, retrieve writing folders, file papers, borrow materials for writing and editing, move to conference areas. At the start of the school year all of this activity probably will distract readers, writers, and their teacher. But since the workshop is silent, or relatively so given the teacher's roving conferences and the quiet voices that kids use in the conference areas, students do learn to block out the scene around them and focus their attention on the task at hand. Since it may take a while to become accustomed to reading and writing in a room with twenty-five other people, this is something that the teacher should talk about with students during the early weeks of the workshop, until they become comfortable with the setting and aren't so distractable. The teacher can also reiterate the reasons that the workshop is silent—because reading and writing are thinking, and because most people need quiet if they're to do their best thinking.

This question also involves issues of discipline and consequences for misbehavior, subjects I avoided in *In the Middle* because every school has its own structures for addressing them. At Boothbay we had an hour-long detention period that teachers supervised on a rotating schedule. If I gave one of my students a deadline for his writing and he did not meet it, he stayed after school, just as he did when he failed to turn in math or science work on time. If a student disrupted the workshop, usually by talking with other kids while not in a conference area, I warned her: "If you talk again today, that's a detention." If the student talked again, and there were no extenuating circumstances, I assigned the detention. I gave about a half dozen detentions each year, most of these in September. Kids learned quickly that I meant business—the workshop was to be used to its maximum potential to break new ground in reading and writing—and I didn't have to fight with them all year about being quiet.

I didn't have perfect students. I did have expectations, standards, and a steely gaze. They knew that I was serious about my commitment to reading and writing because they saw how hard I worked at both, because I decided what was important for them to spend time on in my classroom, and because my collaboration with them as a reader and writer made it possible for them to attain my standards. They understood that twenty finished pieces of writing and thirty-five books were averages from previous years and that I expected them to bear this in mind and be productive. They understood that I wouldn't look at a piece of writing that hadn't already been edited—conscientiously—by the writer. They understood that they had to read real books, not magazines, newspapers, catalogues, or collections of lists. And they understood that I would question them, hard, about the appropriateness of books and pieces of writing that I perceived as racist, sexist, or gratuitously violent.

In fact, I had few negative experiences with eighth graders. From the start I portrayed the workshop as a place where they could grapple with the essential questions of their lives and discover what was possible for them as readers and writers. I honored good writing and reading, but I also honored the kinds of behavior that would lead to it.

I have considered my own variations on the workshop theme since the day I stuffed the manuscript of *In the Middle* into its envelope. The last line of the book contains the observation that workshop teachers must be willing to embrace revision as a way of life, and recently a teacher asked, "If you were writing *In the Middle* today, how would you revise it?"

I would never have used the word *ownership*. Students' *responsibility* for their writing and reading was what I sought, not control for its own sake. I worry that I helped readers infer that in order for students to take ownership of their learning, the teacher has to abdicate ownership of his or her teaching, lower expectations, and let students' choices rule the workshop. I worry most when I get letters from teachers who see themselves as "facilitators" who would avoid "intervening in the learning process."

I intervened all of the time, and I seldom facilitated. I taught. My expectations of my students were enormous, and sometimes my nudges were, in fact, assignments to individual students: "Here, now try this." I also spent time every day demonstrating the options and techniques I wanted kids to try and helping them to demonstrate for each other. The problem with ownership is the implication that any direction or assignment from the teacher is an infringement on students' rights. When I see the stunning writing of Tom Romano's high school students (1987) or Jack Wilde's fifth graders (1985), where the teacher steps in as a writer and reader and directs the range of choice in order to achieve a genuine, well-defined purpose, I wish I could reclaim my manuscript and redefine ownership.

When Tom Newkirk wrote to me about *In the Middle,* he said that for him the key term is *engagement* rather than ownership. I began to recognize what he meant in the work I have undertaken since the book was published. Under a grant from the Bread Loaf School of English, a group of Maine elementary teachers developed models to help students use writing beyond the workshop to learn about other subjects. The range of student choices was necessarily restricted by the content that the children were being asked to learn, so we looked for ways that students could take responsibility and seek engagement within the units of study of a school's math, science, and social studies curricula. Our alternative to the traditional school report borrowed writing workshop methods, and students drafted, revised, edited, and published newspapers, historical fiction, picture books, scripts, poetry, catalogues, calendars, recipe books—in short, reports that informed and engaged them as researchers and actually informed and engaged their readers, too. *Coming to Know* (1990), the book about the project, details our attempts to allow students to bring what they know of writing process to a new situation and create reports that are as personal and meaningful as students' stories of their own experiences.

Coming to Know is also about the uses of academic journals or *learning logs* across the disciplines. I know that if I were writing *In the Middle* today, I would describe the ways that English teachers might use learning logs to pose questions, set themes, and invite students to engage together in brief, first-draft writing about issues that the teacher wants the whole class to explore.

As an English teacher, my experience with whole-group discussions was not positive. I see now how writing in logs gives every student a voice in classroom discourse and helps all students discover what they have to say about a topic. I would assign learning logs in addition to the process-type writing of writing workshop and the dialogue journals of reading workshop, and I would prompt entries whenever I wanted students to think together about an issue related to their writing or their reading— whenever I wanted them to act as researchers.

For example, after a mini-lesson about narrative voice, the teacher might ask students to write for a few minutes in response to the prompt "Who is the narrator of the book you're reading? Why do you think the author chose this narrative voice?" Or when trying to expand kids' awareness of the genres available to writers, a teacher could start by asking them to brainstorm all of the kinds of writing and reading that they can think of. And at the end of each quarter we could ask students to examine their writing and reading of the previous nine weeks and write in their logs, evaluating what they found. In other words, we might explore ways that academic journals can help students become more conscious of what they are doing as writers and readers. I would also use learning logs to create a forum for group talk in the share sessions that end each class: to settle in a circle with our logs and read and talk about what we had written.

What other revisions would I make in my teaching? Recently I learned about the advantages of cross-age tutoring from Elspeth Stuckey, a teacher in South Carolina who directs another of the Bread Loaf projects. I see tremendous benefits in putting middle and secondary school students to work as teachers of younger children. Teachers of adolescents might begin to think about ways to structure regular, sustained contact between groups of older and younger students in the context of workshops, giving their kids opportunities to engage in the enterprise of helping others grow to fluency. My experience as a mother has given me a new perspective on how readers and writers develop and on the social nature of the collaboration that moves a young language learner forward. Through our collaboration my daughter and I both gain understanding. There is a place in junior and senior high schools for adolescents to forge similar relationships, to reflect on their own literacy learning and to put it to use.

Finally, I would add a new appendix to *In the Middle.* During the past few years I have had a wonderful education about children's literature, a genre I ignored as a junior high teacher. The writing in many of the books that I read to my daughter is so fine that I often think about ways that teachers might highlight children's literature for older writers and readers, not so adolescents can write children's books but so that they might learn from how these authors have written.

The brevity of the picture book makes it a perfect form to read aloud and discuss in a mini-lesson. Many of the lessons that English teachers hope student writers will learn are readily apparent in these texts. A teacher might show students how Chris Van Allsburg and Vera B. Williams handled narrative flashbacks in *The Wreck of the Zephyr* and *A Chair for My Mother,* or add Jon Scieszka's *The True Story of the Three Little Pigs* or Janet and Allan Ahlberg's *The Jolly Postman* and *Ten in a Bed* to a collection of material for teaching parody. We could show how an author used poetic language to capture everyday experiences by reading aloud Cynthia Rylant's *When I Was Young in the Mountains*, Tony Johnston's *Yonder*, and Jane Yolen's *Owl Moon*, or share the natural, lively dialogue of *The Ghost-Eye Tree* by Bill Martin, Jr. and John Archambault and *Mirandy and Brother Wind* by Patricia McKissick, or demonstrate a second-person narrative voice by reading Robert McCloskey's *Time of Wonder*. We could illustrate how authors draw on real life for their fiction in such works as *Miss Rumphius* by Barbara Cooney, *The Art Lesson* by Tomie dePaola, and Harriet Ziefert's *A New Coat for Anna*. Or the teacher might read aloud books that represent variations on one theme, for example some of the many versions of the Cinderella story including the Chinese *Yeh-Shen* by Ed Young, the African *Mufaro's Beautiful Daughters* by John Steptoe, *The Egyptian Cinderella* by Shirley Climo, Charlotte Huck's *Princess Furball*, and Babette Cole's parody, *Prince Cinders*.

The books that my daughter and I enjoy are literature. As an adult reader who takes it seriously, I would recommend that teachers introduce children's literature to adolescents as another source of ideas, techniques, inspiration, and pleasure.

The best thing about my letters from teachers is that they show me that I am not unique. Almost every day I hear from teachers who are passionate about writing, reading, and kids. They are problem finders who enjoy observing and theorizing about their teaching and their students' learning. The predictable structure of the workshop has freed them by giving them a stable, authentic context in which to observe and theorize. And it has given students an opportunity to know their teachers as writers and readers. Their success stories show the power of smart, committed, junior high English teachers when they take charge of their professional lives and their curricula.

Dear Nancie,

You may like this observation, and I'll bet that you haven't heard it before. *In the Middle* helped prepare me for job interviews. It helped focus my questions and I was able to lay out how I wanted to teach with plenty of details. Administrators either liked what they heard or they didn't. I didn't want there to be any surprises. And as a result, I think I have a job where administration won't squawk when the main activity in class is reading.

Dear Nancie,

I wonder if anyone has told you that establishing a workshop in her classroom has made her brave. I love the workshop. I love what it has done for me and for my students, and because I really believe in what I am doing, I find myself speaking up in all sorts of situations where I would once have remained silent.

Dear Nancie,

Last spring our school sponsored a workshop, and a spark was ignited. The teachers in our English department each bought a copy of your book and read it at home. The spark turned into a flame! The reaction was unanimous. Our department, made up of teachers ranging in teaching experience from five to almost twenty years, absolutely came alive. It seems each of us was harboring the same doubts and frustrations about vocabulary lists, reading units, and *Warriner's* chapters but we were reluctant to share them with our peers for fear of being perceived as "unprofessional." The entire department met several times during the summer formulating ideas, ordering books (we devoted almost all of our book budget to purchasing class libraries and supplies), designing rooms, and discussing strategies. It is now over a month into the school year, and we are constantly talking in groups about the program, sharing ideas, and supporting each other. *Never* has the English department been so energized.

And the letters show that the workshop is not a fad. It has become a way of life for teachers who understand what they are doing and why.

Dear Nancie,

Right now it's just before noon, and twenty-nine 9th graders are busy at work, writing. So am I. It is our third week of writing workshop and things are already humming. The experience I gained last year, then rereading the book, has left me even better prepared. I *know* now how the workshop approach works; my last year's classes exceeded my wildest expectations, and so far this year looks even better.

My favorite letters in response to *In the Middle* were written by a junior-high teacher in Ticonderoga, New York. Jill Vickers wrote to me the year after *In the Middle* was published and asked if we could arrange to meet and talk at the spring NCTE conference in Boston. She was trying a workshop approach and wrote, "I feel my students are not changing their writing behavior enough and am wondering what more I can do."

I couldn't meet with her. Instead, I suggested that what she might do whenever things weren't going as she would like was to consult with her students, to close her door and talk honestly with her kids about her concerns. Two months later I heard from her again:

Dear Nancie,

Frankly [consult with your students] didn't seem like the kind of profound advice I was hoping for back in the dark days of last winter. . . . However, I feel such a strong tie to the philosophy and behaviors described in your book that I have made a conscious effort to follow your guidelines. So, I took my problems right to my students.

I'll conclude the story with an excerpt from Jill's article (1989) that appeared in *English Journal:*

Part of ownership is sharing the blame when things go awry and seeking solutions. In a mini-lesson, I described, as simply and directly as I could, that the pieces being written were boring. I exaggerated samples I had in my mind and kept them general. The students laughed at how bad the writing could be. Then I asked them what we could do.

Immediately I had to find paper to make a list because there were so many ideas . . . from individual seventh graders who volunteered ways to improve the quality of the writing. Why was I amazed that kids (who'd sat in classes for years analyzing what the teacher was doing wrong) could quickly come up with practical suggestions for improving the quality of their work? Because for years I had been The One doing the thinking, planning, re-thinking, and re-doing based on my best guesses at what was happening (51).

Jill Vickers discovered that she doesn't need Nancie Atwell. She needs her kids: to pay attention to them, to let them lead, and to step in whenever appropriate to instruct them from her own expertise as a writer, reader, and teacher. Jill is one member of the field army of teachers across the country who lead full, literate lives, who sit side by side with kids, discover what feels right for them and their students, and make writing and reading workshops their own.

REFERENCES

AHLBERG, JANET, AND ALLAN AHLBERG. 1986. *The Jolly Postman.* Boston: Little, Brown.

———. 1989. *Ten in a Bed.* New York: Viking Kestrel.

ALIKI. 1986. *How a Book Is Made.* New York: Crowell.

APPLEBEE, ARTHUR. 1978. *The Child's Concept of Story: Ages Two to Seventeen.* Chicago: Chicago University Press.

———. 1987. *Grammar, Punctuation, and Spelling.* Princeton, NJ: National Assessment of Educational Progress.

ATWELL, NANCIE. 1985. "Everyone Sits at a Big Desk: Discovering Topics for Writing." *English Journal* 74 (5): 35–39.

———. 1987. *In the Middle: Writing, Reading and Learning with Adolescents.* Portsmouth, NH: Boynton/Cook.

———, ed. 1990. *Coming to Know: Writing to Learn in the Intermediate Grades.* Portsmouth, NH: Heinemann.

BANG, MOLLY. 1983. *Ten, Nine, Eight.* New York: Greenwillow.

BANKS, LYNNE REID. 1980. *The Indian in the Cupboard.* New York: Avon.

BAYLOR, BYRD. 1986. *I'm in Charge of Celebrations.* New York: Charles Scribner's Sons.

BEMELMANS, LUDWIG. 1939. *Madeline.* New York: Viking Penguin.

BETTELHEIM, BRUNO. 1977. *The Uses of Enchantment: The Meaning and Importance of Fairy Tales.* New York: Alfred A. Knopf.

BISHOP, ELIZABETH. 1983. *The Complete Poems.* New York: Farrar, Straus and Giroux.

BISSEX, GLENDA L., AND RICHARD H. BULLOCK, EDS. 1987. *Seeing for Ourselves: Case-Study Research by Teachers of Writing.* Portsmouth, NH: Heinemann.

BLACKBURN, ELLEN. 1984. "Common Ground: Developing Relationships Between Reading and Writing." *Language Arts* 61 (April): 367–75.

BOTTIGHEIMER, RUTH. 1989. *Grimms' Bad Girls and Bold Boys: The Moral and Social Vision of the "Tales."* New Haven, CT: Yale University Press.

BROWN, MARC. 1987. *D. W. Flips.* Boston: Little, Brown.

BROWN, MARGARET WISE. 1947. *Goodnight Moon.* Harper & Row.

BROWN, REXFORD. 1987. "Who Is Responsible for Thoughtfulness?" *Phi Delta Kappan,* September: 49–52.

BROWN, RUTH. 1981. *A Dark, Dark Tale.* New York: Dial.

BRUNER, JEROME. 1983. *Child's Talk.* New York: Norton.

BUNCE, MARNA. 1989. "Everyday Poets: Recognizing Poetry in Prose." In *Workshop 1: Writing and Literature,* ed. Nancie Atwell. Portsmouth, NH: Heinemann.

CALKINS, LUCY McCORMICK. 1983. *Lessons from a Child: On the Teaching and Learning of Writing.* Portsmouth, NH: Heinemann.

———. 1986. *The Art of Teaching Writing.* Portsmouth, NH: Heinemann.

CAVAFY, C. P. 1975. "The First Step." In *C. P. Cavafy Collected Poems,* trans. Edmund Keeley. Princeton, NJ: Princeton University Press.

CHARLES, DONALD. 1989. *Paddy Pig's Poems.* New York: Simon & Schuster.

CLIMO, SHIRLEY. 1989. *The Egyptian Cinderella.* New York: Thomas Crowell.

COLE, BABETTE. 1987. *Prince Cinders.* London: Picture Lions.

COONEY, BARBARA. 1982. *Miss Rumphius.* New York: Viking Press.

CORMIER, ROBERT. 1978. *I Am the Cheese.* New York: Dell.

CORNELL, ELIZABETH. 1987. "The Effect of Poetry in a First-Grade Classroom." In *Seeing for Ourselves: Case-Study Research by Teachers of Writing,* ed. Glenda L. Bissex and Richard H. Bullock. Portsmouth, NH: Heinemann.

CULLEN, COUNTEE. 1953. "Incident." From *On These I Stand.* New York: Harper & Row.

CUMMINGS, E E. 1940. "anyone lived in a pretty how town." From *Poems 1923–1954.* New York: Harcourt Brace.

DePAOLA, TOMIE. 1989. *The Art Lesson.* New York: G. P. Putnam's Sons.

DE REGNIERS, BEATRICE SCHENK; EVA MOORE; MARY MICHAELS WHITE; AND JAN CARR, EDS. 1988. *Sing a Song of Popcorn.* New York: Scholastic.

DISNEY, WALT. 1986. *Snow White and the Seven Dwarfs.* New York: Gallery Books.

FRANCIS, ROBERT. 1976. "While I Slept." From *Robert Francis: Collected Poems, 1936–1976.* Boston: The University of Massachusetts Press.

FREEMAN, DON. 1968. *Corduroy.* New York: Viking Penguin.

FROST, ROBERT. 1969. *The Poetry of Robert Frost,* ed. Edward Connery Lathem. New York: Henry Holt.

GALDA, LEE. 1988. "Readers, Texts and Context: A Response-Based View of Literature in the Classroom." *The New Advocate* 1 (2) (Spring): 92–102.

GIACOBBE, MARY ELLEN. 1981. "Kids Can Write the First Week of School." *Learning,* September: 132–33.

————. 1986. "Learning to Write and Writing to Learn in the Elementary School." In *The Teaching of Writing: Eighty-fifth Yearbook of the National Society for the Study of Education,* ed. Anthony R. Petrosky and David Bartholomae. Chicago: University of Chicago Press.

————. 1988. "Choosing a Language Arts Textbook." In *Understanding Writing: Ways of Observing, Learning, and Teaching K–8,* 2nd ed, ed. Thomas Newkirk and Nancie Atwell. Portsmouth, NH: Heinemann.

GIOVANNI, NIKKI. 1971. "stars." From *Spin a Soft Black Song.* New York: Farrar, Straus and Giroux.

GOELMAN, HILLEL, ANTOINETTE OBERG, AND FRANK SMITH, EDS. 1984. *Awakening to Literacy.* Portsmouth, NH: Heinemann.

GOODLAD, JOHN. 1984. *A Place Called School.* New York: McGraw-Hill.

GOODMAN, KENNETH. 1987. "Look What They've Done to Judy Blume!: The Basalization of Children's Literature." *The New Advocate* 1 (1) (Fall): 29–41.

GRAVES, DONALD H. 1983. *Writing: Teachers and Children at Work.* Portsmouth, NH: Heinemann.

————. 1990. *Discover Your Own Literacy.* The Reading/Writing Teacher's Companion series. Portsmouth, NH: Heinemann.

GREENFIELD, ELOISE. 1978. *Honey I Love and Other Poems.* New York: Harper Trophy.

HALL, JIM. 1980. "Maybe Dats Youwr Pwoblem Too." From *The Mating Reflex.* Pittsburgh: Carnegie-Mellon University Press.

HANSEN, JANE, THOMAS NEWKIRK, AND DONALD GRAVES, EDS. 1985. *Breaking Ground: Teachers Relate Reading and Writing in the Elementary School.* Portsmouth, NH: Heinemann.

HAUTZIG, DEBORAH. 1986. *The Story of the Nutcracker Ballet.* New York: Random House.

HEARD, GEORGIA. 1989. *For the Good of the Earth and Sun: Teaching Poetry*. Portsmouth, NH: Heinemann.

HINTON, S. E. 1967. *The Outsiders*. New York: Dell.

HOEY, EDWARD. 1966. "Foul Shot." In *Reflections on a Gift of Watermelon Pickle*, ed. Stephen Dunning. Glenview, IL: Scott, Foresman.

HOFF, SYD. 1971. *When Will It Snow?* New York: Harper & Row.

HOPKINS, LEE BENNETT. 1987. *Pass the Poetry Please*. New York: Harper & Row.

HUCK, CHARLOTTE. 1989. *Princess Furball*. New York: Greenwillow.

HUGHES, LANGSTON. 1951. "What Happens to a Dream Deferred?" From *Montage of a Dream Deferred*. New York: Henry Holt.

HUGHES, SHIRLEY. 1973. *Lucy and Tom's Day*. New York: Penguin.

———. 1977. *Dogger*. New York: Lothrop, Lee and Shepard.

———. 1981. *Lucy and Tom's Christmas*. New York: Viking Kestrel.

———. 1982. *Alfie's Feet*. New York: Lothrop, Lee and Shepard.

———. 1985a. *Bathwater's Hot*. New York: Lothrop, Lee and Shepard.

———. 1985b. *When We Went to the Park*. New York: Lothrop, Lee and Shepard.

———. 1987. *Lucy and Tom's 1.2.3*. New York: Viking Kestrel.

HYMES, LUCIA, AND JAMES L. HYMES, JR. 1988. "My Favorite Word." From *Sing a Song of Popcorn*, ed. Beatrice Schenk de Regniers, Eva Moore, Mary Michaels White, and Jan Carr. New York: Scholastic.

JARRELL, RANDALL. 1968. "The Woman at the Washington Zoo." In *Randall Jarrell: The Complete Poems*. New York: Farrar.

JOHNSTON, TONY. 1988. *Yonder*. New York: Dial Books.

KENNEDY, X. J., AND DOROTHY KENNEDY. 1982. *Knock at a Star: A Child's Introduction to Poetry*. Boston: Little, Brown.

KERR, JUDITH. 1968. *The Tiger Who Came to Tea*. London: Picture Lions.

KIDDER, TRACY. 1989. *Among Schoolchildren*. Boston: Houghton Mifflin.

KOCH, KENNETH. 1970. *Wishes, Lies and Dreams*. New York: Vintage.

KOCH, KENNETH, AND KATE FARRELL, EDS. 1985. *Talking to the Sun*. New York: Henry Holt.

KOOSER, TED. 1969. "Child Frightened by a Thunderstorm." From *Official Entry Blank*. Omaha: University of Nebraska Press.

KRAUSS, RUTH. 1945. *The Carrot Seed*. New York: Harper & Row.

LEE, DENNIS. 1983. "The Puzzle." From *Jelly Belly*. Toronto: Macmillan.

LEE, HARPER. 1960. *To Kill a Mockingbird*. Philadelphia: Lippincott.

LEVERTOV, DENISE. 1966. "What Were They Like?" In *The Sorrow Dance*. New York: New Directions.

LEVINSON, RIKI. 1985. *Watch the Stars Come Out*. New York: E. P. Dutton.

———. 1986. *I Go with My Family to Grandma's*. New York: E. P. Dutton.

LEWIS, C. S. 1950. *The Lion, the Witch and the Wardrobe*. New York: Macmillan.

LLOYD, DAVID. 1986. *The Stopwatch*. New York: Harper Trophy.

LLOYD, PAMELA. 1987. *How Writers Write*. Portsmouth, NH: Heinemann.

LONGFELLOW, HENRY WADSWORTH. 1983. *Hiawatha*. Illus. Susan Jeffers. New York: Dial.

McCARTHY, MARY. 1954. *A Charmed Life*. New York: Harcourt Brace Jovanovich.

McCLOSKEY, ROBERT. 1952. *One Morning in Maine*. New York: Viking Press.

———. 1957. *Time of Wonder*. New York: Viking Press.

McKISSICK, PATRICIA. 1988. *Mirandy and Brother Wind*. New York: Alfred A. Knopf.

MARTIN, BILL, JR. 1967. *Brown Bear, Brown Bear, What Do You See?* New York: Holt, Rinehart and Winston.

MARTIN, BILL, JR., AND JOHN ARCHAMBAULT. 1985. *The Ghost-Eye Tree*. New York: Henry Holt and Co.

———. 1987. *Here Are My Hands*. New York: Henry Holt and Co.

MAYER, MERCER. 1985. *Just Grandpa and Me*. New York: Western.

MELSER, JUNE, AND JOY COWLEY. 1980. *Yes Ma'am*. Bothell, WA: The Wright Group.

MINARIK, ELSE HOLMELUND. 1960. *Little Bear's Friend*. New York: Harper & Row.

MURRAY, DONALD M. 1982. *Learning by Teaching: Selected Articles on Writing and Teaching*. Portsmouth, NH: Boynton/Cook.

———. 1985. *A Writer Teaches Writing*. 2nd ed. Boston: Houghton Mifflin.

———. 1986. *Read to Write*. Fort Worth: Holt, Rinehart and Winston.

———. 1990. *Write to Learn*. 3rd ed. Fort Worth: Holt, Rinehart and Winston.

NEWKIRK, THOMAS. 1989. *More Than Stories: The Range of Children's Writing*. Portsmouth, NH: Heinemann.

———. 1990. "Looking for Trouble: A Way to Unmask Our Readings." In *To Compose: Teaching Writing in High School and College*. 2nd ed. Portsmouth, NH: Heinemann.

NEWKIRK, THOMAS, AND NANCIE ATWELL, EDS. 1988. *Understanding Writing: Ways of Observing, Learning, and Teaching K–8.* 2nd ed. Portsmouth, NH: Heinemann.

NEWMAN, JUDITH, ED. 1985. *Whole Language: Theory in Use.* Portsmouth, NH: Heinemann.

O'DELL, SCOTT. 1977. *Sing Down the Moon.* New York: Dell.

PAPERT, SEYMOUR. 1980. *Mindstorms: Children, Computers, and Powerful Ideas.* New York: Basic Books.

PATERSON, KATHERINE. 1977. *Bridge to Terabithia.* New York: Avon.

———. 1989. *The Spying Heart.* New York: E. P. Dutton.

PEPPÉ, RODNEY. 1970. *The House That Jack Built.* New York: Delacorte Press.

PIERCY, MARGE. 1982. *Circles on the Water: Selected Poems of Marge Piercy.* New York: Alfred A. Knopf.

———. 1982. "What's that Smell in the Kitchen?" In *Circles on the Water: Selected Poems of Marge Piercy.* New York: Alfred A. Knopf.

RIEF, LINDA. 1989. "Seeking Diversity: Reading and Writing from the Middle to the Edge." In *Workshop 1: Writing and Literature,* ed. Nancie Atwell. Portsmouth, NH: Heinemann.

ROMANO, TOM. 1987. *Clearing the Way: Working with Teenage Writers.* Portsmouth, NH: Heinemann.

ROSENBLATT, LOUISE. 1938; 1976. *Literature as Exploration.* New York: Noble and Noble.

RUTSALA, VERN. 1978. "The Mill Back Home." From *Walking Home from the Icehouse.* Pittsburgh: Carnegie-Mellon University Press.

RYLANT, CYNTHIA. 1982. *When I Was Young in the Mountains.* New York: E. P. Dutton.

———. 1984. *Waiting to Waltz.* New York: Bradbury Press.

———. 1990. *The Soda Jerk.* New York: Bradbury Press.

SCIESZKA, JON. 1989. *The True Story of the Three Little Pigs.* New York: Viking Kestrel.

SELSAM, MILLICENT. 1946. *From Egg to Chick.* New York: Harper Trophy.

SENDAK, MAURICE. 1963. *Where the Wild Things Are.* New York: Harper & Row.

———. 1981. *Outside over There.* New York: Harper & Row.

SIMIC, CHARLES. 1971. "Stone." From *Dismantling the Silence.* New York: George Braziller.

SMITH, FRANK. 1978. *Reading Without Nonsense.* New York: Teachers College Press.

———. 1983. *Essays into Literacy: Selected Papers and Some Afterthoughts.* Portsmouth, NH: Heinemann.

———. 1988. "Reading Like a Writer." In *Joining the Literacy Club: Further Essays into Education.* Portsmouth, NH: Heinemann.

STEIG, WILLIAM. 1969. *Sylvester and the Magic Pebble.* New York: Simon & Schuster.

STEPTOE, JON. 1987. *Mufaro's Beautiful Daughters.* New York: Lothrop, Lee and Shepard.

STEVENS, WALLACE. 1951. "The Noble Rider and the Sound of Words." In *The Necessary Angel: Essays on Reality and the Imagination.* New York: Alfred A. Knopf.

STIRES, SUSAN. 1983a. "Disabled Writers: A Positive Approach." In *Teaching All the Children to Write,* ed. James Collins. Buffalo, NY: New York State English Council.

———. 1983b. "Real Audiences and Contexts for LD Writers." *Academic Therapy,* May: 67–75.

SWOPE, SAM. 1989. *The Araboolies of Liberty Street.* New York: Clarkson Potter.

TITHERINGTON, JEANNE. 1985. *Big World, Small World.* New York: Greenwillow.

———. 1987. *A Place for Ben.* New York: Greenwillow.

TROUSDALE, ANN. 1989. "Let the Children Tell Us: The Meanings of Fairy Tales for Children." *The New Advocate* 2 (1) (Winter): 37–48.

UPDIKE, JOHN. 1965. *A Child's Calendar.* New York: Alfred A. Knopf.

VAN ALLSBURG, CHRIS. 1983. *The Wreck of the Zephyr.* Boston: Houghton Mifflin.

———. 1986. *The Stranger.* Boston: Houghton Mifflin.

VICKERS, JILL. 1989. In "A Symposium: Teachers in the Middle." *English Journal* 78 (1) (January): 51.

VYGOTSKY, LEV S. 1962. *Thought and Language.* Cambridge, MA: MIT Press.

———. 1978. *Mind in Society: The Development of Higher Psychological Processes.* Cambridge, MA: Harvard University Press.

WALLACE, ROBERT. 1987. *Writing Poems.* 2nd ed. Boston: Little, Brown.

WALLACE, RONALD. 1983. "You Can't Write a Poem About McDonald's." From *Tunes for Bears to Dance to.* Pittsburgh: University of Pittsburgh Press.

WELLS, GORDON. 1986. *The Meaning Makers: Children Learning Language and Using Language to Learn.* Portsmouth, NH: Heinemann.

WILDE, JACK. 1985. "Play, Power, and Plausibility: The Growth of Fiction Writers." In *Breaking Ground: Teachers Relate Reading and Writing in the Elementary School,* ed. Jane Hansen, Thomas Newkirk, and Donald Graves. Portsmouth, NH: Heinemann.

———. 1989. Interview by Thomas Newkirk. In *Workshop 1: Writing and Literature,* ed. Nancie Atwell. Portsmouth, NH: Heinemann.

WILLIAMS, VERA B. 1982. *A Chair for My Mother.* New York: Greenwillow Books.

———. 1983. *Something Special for Me*. New York: Greenwillow.

YOLEN, JANE. 1987. *Owl Moon*. New York: Philomel.

YOUNG, ED. 1982. *Yeh-Shen*. New York: Philomel.

ZIEFERT, HARRIET. *A New Coat for Anna*. 1986. New York: Alfred A. Knopf.

ZINSSER, WILLIAM. 1987. *Inventing the Truth: The Art of Memoir*. Boston: Houghton Mifflin.

———. 1990. *On Writing Well*. 4th ed. New York: Harper & Row.